Questions in Aest

*Introductory Studies in Philosophy of Education*
*Series Editors:* PHILIP SNELDERS and COLIN WRINGE

*Education and the Value of Knowledge*
M. A. B. Degenhardt

*Can We Teach Children To Be Good?*
Roger Straughan

*Means and Ends in Education*
Brenda Cohen

*Mixed Ability Grouping: A Philosophical Perspective*
Charles Bailey and David Bridges

*The Education of Feeling and Emotion*
Francis Dunlop

*Democracy, Schooling and Political Education*
Colin Wringe

*Religious Education: Philosophical Perspectives*
John Sealey

*Freedom and Discipline*
Richard Smith

# Questions in Aesthetic Education

H. B. REDFERN

London
ALLEN & UNWIN
Boston       Sydney

© H. B. Redfern, 1986
This book is copyright under the Berne Convention. No reproduction without permission. All rights reserved.

**Allen & Unwin (Publishers) Ltd,**
**40 Museum Street, London WC1A 1LU, UK**

Allen & Unwin (Publishers) Ltd,
Park Lane, Hemel Hempstead, Herts HP2 4TE, UK

Allen & Unwin, Inc.,
8 Winchester Place, Winchester, Mass. 01890, USA

Allen & Unwin (Australia) Ltd,
8 Napier Street, North Sydney, NSW 2060, Australia

First published in 1986

---

**British Library Cataloguing in Publication Data**

Redfern, H. B.
   Questions in aesthetic education. – (Introductory studies in philosophy of education)
   1. Aesthetics – Study and Teaching
   I. Title   II. Series
   111′.85′07   BH61
   ISBN 0–04–370162–0
   ISBN 0–04–370163–9 Pbk

---

**Library of Congress Cataloging in Publication Data**

Redfern, H. B. (Hildred Betty)
   Questions in aesthetic education.
   (Introductory studies in philosophy of education)
   Bibliography: p.
   Includes index.
   I. Aesthetics – Study and teaching.   I. Title.
II. Series.
BH61.R43 1986   111′.85′07   85–18554
ISBN 0–04–370–162–0 (alk. paper)
ISBN 0–04–370–163–9 (pbk. : alk. paper)

---

Set in 11 on 12 point Plantin by
Phoenix Photosetting of Chatham
and printed and bound in Great Britain by
Biddles Ltd, Guildford and King's Lynn

# Contents

|   | | |
|---|---|---|
| | Editors' Foreword | *page* ix |
| | Preface | xi |
| 1 | Introduction | 1 |
| 2 | How Is the Aesthetic Related to Art? | 14 |
| 3 | The Concept of Art | 31 |
| 4 | Imagination, Feeling and Aesthetic Education | 45 |
| 5 | Aesthetic Education in the Arts | 67 |
| 6 | Aesthetic Education outside the Arts | 97 |
| | Further Reading | 111 |
| | References | 114 |
| | Index | 119 |

## Editors' Foreword

Books that are available to students of philosophy of education may, in general, be divided into two types. There are collections of essays and articles making up a more or less random selection; and there are books which explore a single theme or argument in depth but, having been written to break new ground, are often unsuitable for general readers or those near the beginning of their course. The Introductory Studies in Philosophy of Education are intended to fill what is widely regarded as an important gap in this range.

The series aims to provide a collection of short, readable works which, besides being philosophically sound, will seem relevant and accessible to future and existing teachers without a previous knowledge of philosophy or of philosophy of education. In the planning of the series account has necessarily been taken of the tendency of present-day courses of teacher education to follow a more integrated and less discipline-based pattern than formerly. Account has also been taken of the fact that students on three- and four-year courses, as well as those on shorter postgraduate and in-service courses, quite understandably expect their theoretical studies to have a clear bearing on their practical concerns, and on their dealings with children. Each book, therefore, starts from a real and widely recognized problem in the education field, and explores the main philosophical approaches which illuminate and clarify it, or suggests a coherent standpoint even when it does not claim to provide a solution. Attention is paid to the work of both mainstream philosophers and philosophers of education. For students who wish to pursue particular questions in depth, each book contains a bibliographical essay or a substantial list of suggestions for further reading. It is intended that a full range of the main topics recently discussed by philosophers of education should eventually be covered by the series.

Besides having considerable experience in the teaching of

philosophy of education, the majority of the authors writing in the series have already received some recognition in their particular fields. In addition, therefore, to reviewing and criticizing existing work, each author has his or her own positive contribution to make to further discussion.

In *Questions in Aesthetic Education* Betty Redfern argues that within the thinking of many educationists today aesthetic education is a somewhat amorphous notion which makes both for widespread theoretical confusion and for practical shortcomings in many classrooms, art and dance studios, and so forth.

As what is still mainly a philosopher's concept, she insists, the aesthetic requires for its clarification some understanding of its relatively short but troubled history together with a careful examination of such related concepts as 'beauty', 'art', 'imagination', 'form', and 'pleasure'. In addition, elucidation is needed of certain others with which the idea of the aesthetic has become associated within the context of education – in particular, 'creativity' and 'expression of feeling'. Misunderstandings that arise in connection with these, it is suggested, often make for an imbalance in arts education, namely, in terms of making and doing at the expense of critical appreciation and reasoned reflection. Such appreciation and reflection, however, Dr Redfern claims, extend beyond the arts to other areas, including that of everyday life, and deserve more serious consideration than they currently receive.

Philip Snelders<br>
Colin Wringe

# Preface

As the title indicates, this book is primarily of an exploratory nature and, although certain suggestions are put forward by way of possible answers to most of the questions raised they are necessarily provisional and incomplete. Strictly, it should be entitled '*Some* questions in aesthetic education'; for the field is vast, and only a limited selection of problems can be considered within an introductory text of this length. Moreover, both as a subject of theoretical investigation and as a practical enterprise aesthetic education is enormously complex and demanding, and the book will have succeeded in part if it does no more than counter what seems to be a growing assumption that this is an area where anyone, indeed everyone, may dabble. Rather, it is the case that while many may *think* they are engaged in the undertaking, and talk rather lightly of 'the aesthetic', relatively few appear to have given serious thought to what it might involve.

There is thus a need for a better grasp, first, of the nature and scope of the problems within the discipline of philosophical aesthetics; and, second, of the challenges facing practitioners in the field and of how the two sets of problems are interconnected. Chapters 2, 3 and 4 focus on the former; 1, 5 and 6 on the latter. But it cannot be emphasized too strongly that this preliminary foray (which remains within the parameters of analytical philosophy) risks over-simplifying and even distorting the issues discussed and their treatment by writers of some distinction. Study of primary sources and further reading are therefore essential – ideally, under the guidance of a professional philosopher with knowledge and experience in this realm.

I am grateful to Dance Books Ltd for permission to draw on some of the material from my book *Dance, Art and Aesthetics* (1983).

H. B. Redfern<br>
*January 1985*

# 1

# *Introduction*

It is perhaps no exaggeration to claim that in both educational practice and theory there is more confusion about aesthetic education than about any other area of the curriculum. A great deal of what is to be found in the educational literature, not least in official reports and inquiries, is apt to be vague, riddled with misconceptions and unwarranted assumptions, and sometimes sheer nonsense. Why might this be?

In the first place there is the difficulty of what is to be understood by the term 'aesthetic education' and what falls under that heading. Yet this is a problem that scarcely seems to be recognized, let alone explored, by many who freely employ the concept. On the contrary, as Alan Simpson (1983) points out, 'aesthetic' has come to be used in the educational context as a bland, inoffensive label, a term now absorbed into and sanctified by official usage. Nothing could be more ironic, for ever since it first evolved in the eighteenth century the aesthetic has been a problematic concept. But it is one that is far too important to be treated casually, and certainly not in a field itself as important and controversial as education.

In the main it seems to be taken for granted that aesthetic education is somehow connected with, though not restricted to, the arts. But the nature of that connection is seldom questioned, much less thoroughly investigated. Thus the DES publication *Curriculum 11–16* (1977), for example, baldly declares that 'Clearly art is central to the aesthetic area' (p. 36) without apparently any awareness that, far from being clear, this is a highly debatable issue – as too is the question of whether the aesthetic is central to art. And if 'art' refers here only to the visual arts, then it is again a doubtful assertion; for on what grounds are these art forms to be considered nearer to the heart of the aesthetic than, say, music, poetry, or the dance?

By contrast, the DES survey *Primary Education in England* (1978), having stated that 'Aesthetic education may arise in connection with work in any area of the curriculum' (para. 5.85), goes on to consider music, along with art and craft, under the heading 'aesthetic and physical education'. These subjects, it is claimed, 'contribute particularly to the development of children's aesthetic response through making and doing, looking and listening, touching and moving'. But, like so many statements in such reports, it is unclear whether this is intended to be taken as an empirical claim established by large-scale observation and experiment, or as stating a conceptual truth: that, of their nature, these subjects are the ones that must necessarily make such a contribution, that things could not be otherwise.

Certainly, from what is said later in this survey it would appear that music is to be included in the curriculum chiefly in virtue of its status as art; yet at the same time it seems to be valued in English primary schools less for its intrinsic worth than as a useful adjunct to the conduct of the daily assembly in general and the act of worship in particular. Even more markedly, painting and drawing are discussed here less as arts than as a means of recording information, illustrating historical events and the like. Of course, drawing, painting, modelling and a whole variety of activities might be used to assist understanding of other subject areas; and such work might – though it need not – have aesthetic significance (as we shall see). But can aesthetic education, or more precisely, arts education, seriously be in hand when the main concern is something else – especially something involving matters of truth to fact?

Again, while the dance has in more recent years made notable progress in education as an art form in its own right, it is still often treated as part of that multifarious and ever-expanding collection of activities known – not at all satisfactorily, many might agree – as 'physical education'. But neither is drama nor literature mentioned in the sections on aesthetic education of *Primary Education in England* and *Education 5–9* (DES, 1982a). Nor, as in *Curriculum 11–16*, are they considered first and foremost as arts, but rather as a means of acquiring linguistic and social skills, that is, chiefly in instrumental terms. It might, however, be noted that the phrase 'literature *and* the fine arts' (my italics) sometimes occurs outside, as well as inside, educational discourse. On the other hand – a point of major significance, I shall maintain – it is customary to distinguish *imaginative* literature from, for example, biography and travel writing.

Then what of that interest and delight, often assumed to be an aesthetic interest and delight, and sometimes touched on in official reports, in the colours, patterns, textures, rhythms, proportions and forms of things outside art – for example, on the nature table or in the laboratory, in gardens, parks and city squares, among mountains or by the sea? Or, similarly, in the case of cars, aeroplanes, bridges, and so on (we might recall mention in Rupert Brooke's poem *The Great Lover* of 'the keen / Unpassioned beauty of a great machine')? Indeed, *Curriculum 11-16* speaks of aesthetic 'skills' that are to be developed in craft, design and technology courses (p. 33). And should opportunities for aesthetic experience offered by other areas of the curriculum be seized on by teachers, or should any such interest that arises be regarded as simply fortuitous – a bonus, as it were, that may be left to take care of itself?

However, reference in *Primary Education in England* to 'touching and moving' raises the question of whether, and if so how, an aesthetic response is to be distinguished from one that is merely sensuous; and, if there is no difference, how there could be *education* in this realm. For, if an individual does not enjoy the sensation of, for instance, handling wet clay or whirling round and then flopping to the ground, there is little that can be learned here that might modify or change such reactions any more than in the case of liking or disliking, say, the flavour of aniseed or the smell of newly mown hay. Any idea of improvement or development would seem out of place.

If, further (again sometimes mentioned in the official literature), aesthetic considerations enter into matters to do with, say, dress (including, of course, school uniform); the way pupils and teachers take meals (for example, the layout of tables, the manner of eating and drinking); how individuals sit, walk and generally move about; the appearance and treatment of books, equipment, notice-boards and the school building as a whole – if, that is, there is what Roger Scruton (1979) calls 'an aesthetics of everyday life' – is it to be expected that experience of the arts (for example) automatically carries over to wider contexts? And can there be any justification for teachers caring about and taking responsibility for aesthetic education within the arts but not in the everyday sphere (assuming for the moment that arts education does involve the aesthetic)?

A common misconception that becomes especially evident in this connection, though it is one that is to some extent understandable in the light of the history of the concept of the aesthetic, is that aesthetic awareness is equivalent to an awareness of beauty. This is implied, for instance, in *Curriculum 11-16* in the statement following that which alleges that art is central to the aesthetic: 'but to confine it there, in the "pursuit of the beautiful", is a serious limitation with overtones of dilettantism' (p. 36). Certainly if there were such equivalence this would be seriously limiting – and not only in respect of the arts, but any object of aesthetic interest. However, this would seem to be confusing the aesthetic with *aestheticism* – aestheticism, at any rate, in one of its senses (discussed in the next chapter).

A similarly mistaken conception of the aesthetic is apparent in the DES publication *Aesthetic Development* (1982b), prepared by the exploratory group set up to advise the Assessment of Performance Unit on this subject (which I shall sometimes refer to as the APU document). Yet even in the eighteenth century, when early aesthetic theory tended to be dominated by the idea of the beautiful, there was never any identifying of the two concepts; and any such conflation would be rejected by most twentieth-century scholars, as well as, in the case of the arts, by many artists and critics. Moreover, contrary to what the authors of *Aesthetic Development* seem to assume (para. 2.2), to appraise something as ugly (or unsightly, hideous, garish, etc.) is to take an aesthetic standpoint no less than in the case of appraising something as beautiful (or elegant, graceful, pretty, etc.); and again this is consistent with traditional aesthetic thought. Like moral appraisals, aesthetic appraisals may be favourable or unfavourable.

INTRODUCTION

A related question here is whether there is a distinctive class of aesthetic concepts or aesthetic features, such as loveliness or ugliness, as opposed to a distinctive class of non-aesthetic concepts or features, such as roundness, smoothness or verticality.

A further source of confusion in educational discourse is the regular coupling of 'aesthetic' with 'creative', yet usually with no attempt either to explain or justify this conjunction. Thus in *Curriculum 11-16* 'the aesthetic and creative' is picked out as one of the areas of experience that it is recommended should form the compulsory curriculum for pupils of this age group; and this is then taken up in the Calouste Gulbenkian Foundation's Inquiry, *The Arts in Schools* (1982), in which 'the aesthetic and creative' is referred to as 'a distinct category of understanding' – a bold and indeed contentious claim on account of its epistemological character (that is, having to do with knowledge) and therefore requiring justification.

The aesthetic is certainly one of several modes of awareness which for over two centuries has been held to be irreducible to any other (traditionally it was contrasted in particular with moral and scientific awareness), though this is not to say that it has necessarily been seen as logically independent of all other knowledge. But to link it with 'the creative' suggests that something else is required to establish a distinct realm of experience. Moreover, the concept of creativity – which, by contrast with that of the aesthetic, has received a good deal of attention in relation to education – is itself one of some complexity. It is, indeed, as R. K. Elliott (1971) has argued, 'a concept with an eventful history' (p. 144), and its application does not necessarily involve either art or the aesthetic. In much of the literature on aesthetic and arts education, however, insufficient note appears to have been taken of the various senses of the terms 'creative', 'creativeness', etc., which Elliott usefully distinguishes, and there is often a confused and confusing slipping to and fro between those senses. In the main, however, 'the aesthetic and creative' seems intended to indicate participation in activities such as writing one's own poems, stories and plays; painting and drawing; modelling, sculpting and other work of a three-dimensional kind; dancing; music-making; dramatic improvization and mime; and so on – activities, that is, which may be (and perhaps typically are) pursued as artistic activities but which, as hinted at earlier, need not be.

It might, then, be supposed that '. . . and creative' is meant to draw attention to what is seen as the desirability of arts education extending beyond 'merely' looking, listening and reading imaginative literature, though any case for this usually remains largely unargued. And it soon becomes obvious from further perusal of most official publications that 'creative' work is indeed regarded as not only indispensable but central to the whole enterprise – indeed, to the whole of aesthetic education. Hence the widespread talk of 'the creative arts', 'the performing arts', and – importing yet another problematic idea into the arena – 'the expressive arts'. A further illustration of the muddle that exists in connection with the subject is Maurice Holt's division in *The Common Curriculum* between 'creative activities', understood as art and craft, and 'the expressive domain and the humanities'.

Sometimes it is even recommended that arts education should consist almost entirely of 'participation' in the narrow sense of 'making and doing'. *Curriculum 11-16*, for instance, under the heading 'Art' expressly states that for this age-group the study of art 'is essentially, if not wholly, a practical activity' (p. 37); and once more the stress is on the faithful *recording* of how things are (the very antithesis of being 'creative', in whatever sense that slippery term is understood). The mind of not only any civilized but any fair-minded person must surely reel. Are the majority of young people really to leave school with scarcely any introduction to at least some of the great works of painting and sculpture (and, by extension, to music, drama, etc.) and so be denied the opportunity of having a basis even for declining further acquaintance? Are they to be left to find their own way about among the vast range of art forms and crafts, or perhaps (since to understand contemporary achievements some sense of historical perspective is needed) miss it altogether? Are they to have no guidance in respect of standards and no knowledge or experience of critical reflection other than that which (it is to be hoped) applies to their own endeavours? The *Education 5-9* survey, which does recognize the vital importance of discussion with children of at least what they themselves produce or read 'for pleasure', depressingly reports 'relatively few' instances of such discussion (para. 2.14); while the practice of reading poetry to pupils of both this and older age-groups seems to have declined considerably.

Furthermore, what of those arts which are not typically or easily engaged in as practical activities in schools, but which are the most widely available, namely the arts of television, radio and cinema? Considering all the talk about imagination in connection with aesthetic education, it is curious, to say the least, that radio drama, which stimulates image-making in a wholly unique way, releasing the individual from the tyranny of visual images presented by others, and which, through outstanding writers such as Arden, Beckett, Bolt, Orton and Pinter, has significantly influenced all other forms of drama (including drama-documentary) for almost half a century – has, indeed, kept poetry and the *literary* use of language in general intensely alive in the theatre – should so consistently be ignored.

What also of the appreciation of architecture, which surrounds us everywhere and about which an educated person might be expected to be able to express a thoughtful opinion? How many among the crowds of people who today visit cathedrals, churches, castles, stately homes and the like are able to take a serious aesthetic interest in what they see, including too the art treasures often displayed, the landscaped gardens, the surrounding countryside or townscape? If but few, is not this largely owing to the imbalance that persists in many schools between doing and making, on the one hand, and learning to look and listen imaginatively on the other?

Both the APU document and *The Arts in Schools* (which I shall be referring to frequently in view of their attempts to move away somewhat from much of the dogma that has prevailed for so long in this area of educational 'theory') do urge the importance of what is commonly called 'appreciation', as set over against (though rather oddly) what seems to be known as 'participation'. The *Aesthetic Development* publication has, indeed, the courage to suggest that, especially in some art forms, there tends to be too great an emphasis on creative work (though the added remark 'to the exclusion of considering how much there is to be learned from some of the great works of art' is perhaps, as I shall discuss in later chapters, a rather doubtful way of making what is nevertheless a very important point – para. 4.4.3).

The issue has been aired briefly by J. P. White (1973), who mentions the visual arts in particular, especially in the case of the 'less able' child. But the question he raises of whether participation in creative activity is necessary at all for an understanding and love of the arts is rarely, if ever, referred to in official publications, let alone debated. Rather, it is either taken for granted or else simply prescribed. Thus *The Arts in Schools* simply asserts that 'participation and appreciation are complementary aspects of art education' (para. 58). No doubt they *can* complement each other and, where both are included, should; but whether there *ought* to be creative activity for purposes of aesthetic education within a compulsory curriculum is a prior question. What is merely an expression of opinion, and with that an implied recommendation, is presented here, rather, as if it were an undeniable truth. Similarly with the added claim that 'to opt for one at the expense of the other will impoverish both'. But how does anyone know that lack of experience in, say, 'creative writing' or 'creative dance' impoverishes literary or dance appreciation? Again, neither argument nor evidence is offered.

Any attempt to understand why such stress is placed on doing and making in the name of aesthetic or arts education requires an awareness of the web of confusion and mistaken beliefs not only about the concepts of art, the aesthetic and creativity, but also about what are usually assumed to be necessarily related concepts such as expression, communication, feeling and imagination – each of which, however, is many-stranded and in need of some unravelling. For instance, what sort or sorts of expression or feeling – if any – are involved in aesthetic and artistic experience? Is the work of a creative artist much the same as his having a good laugh or a good cry, or in some way an outer reflection of what is 'within' – if, indeed, such an idea makes any *sense*? What are we to make of talk about the various arts as languages? How is aesthetic imagination to be distinguished from a historical or scientific or philosophical imagination (and is this the best or even a sensible way of posing the problem)? What of that distinction to which Coleridge drew attention in the *Biographia Literaria* (ch. 13) between imagination and fantasy ('fancy', as he called it), yet which is totally ignored, or not even recognized, in most educational literature?

All too often blanket references to *the* imagination, creativity, inventiveness, problem-solving and the like are to be found which involve a failure to realize that such capacities can properly be understood only in terms of specific achievements in fields that may be as various as theoretical physics, figure-skating, political diplomacy and music. The myth still persists among many people in education that there are certain mental qualities or abilities of a general kind that are capable of being cultivated through one type of activity or study and then used in others. Thus, the Introduction to the Gulbenkian *Report on Dance Education* (1980) proclaims that 'Britain's richest resource is neither oil nor coal but the imagination of her people', and then goes on to state that 'This imagination is most stirred and developed through education in the arts. The arts . . . are a way of having ideas, of *training* the imagination' (p. VIII, my italics). Similarly, there is often a lack of recognition that talk of fostering 'sensitivity and awareness' through the arts requires prior consideration of the questions: Sensitivity to what? Awareness of what? For sensitivity to, say, the poetic use of language or imagery is hardly to be equated with moral sensitivity; nor awareness of a change of musical key with awareness of another person's mood.

A further set of questions has to do with why, anyway, the aesthetic mode of experience – if it *is* a discrete mode – might be thought of importance in education, and what might be its aims. It is frequently claimed on behalf of the arts, for example – as also for sport, design and technology courses, etc. – that they have a contribution to make to moral and social development, to personal and interpersonal understanding, to growth of the whole person and self-realization, to the learning of other subjects (either directly or by acting as 'balancers'), and, perhaps above all, to the affective life of the individual. Indeed, John Wilson (1978) identifies aesthetic education as a subsection of the education of the emotions. Unless, however, it can be shown that a subject is *of its very nature* concerned with certain aspects of understanding and development, it has no greater claim to a place in a common curriculum than others which may have similar fortuitous consequences; and of course it does not have as good a claim as a subject which necessarily involves the particular kind of understanding or development in question.

This is not to deny that, for example, the study of some kinds of literature might lead to increased moral sensitivity, or that participation in some kinds of dancing might help to promote interpersonal understanding. But, if such possibilities are set up as aims, the artistic character of the activity is likely to be distorted. Thus, to say that drama is 'predominantly a means to explore social attitudes, personal relationships, inner conflict' (*Curriculum 11–16*, p. 39) is to characterize it as a curriculum activity in *non*-artistic terms. Aesthetic awareness is in fact almost wholly discounted in this section of the publication: it is explicitly stated that the bodily and linguistic skills to be developed are 'social skills, not graces' (a questionable distinction, however). The authors none the less want it both, indeed several, ways, for they can hardly leave out all mention of 'appreciation of good plays and theatre', though not under 'Essentials'; and, in addition, they conclude by referring to enjoyment – this 'above all, perhaps' (p. 41).

The question of enjoyment can hardly be avoided in connection with aesthetic education and will be examined in some detail in Chapter 4; but meantime we might note Ruth Saw's distinction between enjoying something and enjoying *oneself* in its presence: 'It may be very pleasant to sit and daydream while the orchestra makes pleasant sounds', she says, 'but that is not to enjoy the music' (1972, p. 60).

Questions about aims and values give rise, in turn, to the question of assessment (to use that term in a general sense); for to have an aim presupposes a result and the possibility of checking that result. If, for example, to stay with the case of drama, a teacher's prime concern is not with aesthetic or artistic values, but with fostering understanding of personal relationships, it must be in terms of such understanding that dramatic activity is evaluated: enjoyment of acting, say, or increased appreciation of language will not be enough, since such enjoyment and appreciation would not be incompatible with a pupil's repeatedly behaving quite inappropriately in relation to others or with his misunderstanding the nature of certain relationships between other people, whether in real life or as portrayed in a simulated situation.

What, then, are the criteria of excellence that apply in the aesthetic realm? Or is it inappropriate to think in terms of a set of such criteria specifiable in advance of particular cases? What counts as aesthetic development? How is the concept of art acquired? To what extent, if at all, is technique to be regarded as important in making and doing; and are there any skills that might be acquired for 'appreciation'? How is the mere passing on of the preferences of particular teachers or a particular section of society to be avoided – if, indeed, it can be? And should such preferences be made known to the pupils?

The foregoing questions are but a sample of many connected with aesthetic education that confront teachers and their advisers, whether they recognize them or not. They have been selected here because they seem to be the most fundamental; and, although some might be illuminated by reference to the history of ideas, while others raise further issues that require investigation by psychology and sociology, they are all inescapably philosophical. For philosophical inquiry is concerned, among other things, with scrutinizing what is presupposed by the various categories of thought and experience with which we operate, and with making those presuppositions explicit; with establishing whether various remarks are meaningful or not and, if they are, elucidating that meaning; hence with analysing concepts and showing their relationships with other concepts; with questioning also the nature of statements and claims (whether, for instance, they are empirical or conceptual), and what conditions have to be satisfied to know whether what someone says is true or false, defensible or indefensible.

If, for example, terms such as 'aesthetic', 'creative', 'expressive', and 'imaginative' are bandied about indiscriminately, those attempting to discuss aesthetic education are likely to misunderstand one another; worse, they will literally not know what they are talking about. Nor can empirical inquiry into, say, creativity or imagination usefully proceed unless there is a prior clarification of such concepts: before anything can be explained or tested it has to be identified and described.

We are also necessarily involved in philosophy whenever we consider the values of an area of study or experience and the claims put forward on its behalf in a particular field such as education. A reasoned justification of aesthetic and artistic pursuits, especially within a compulsory curriculum, is clearly a matter of utmost importance – the more so since, as I have indicated, they are apt to suffer from the grandiose yet often incoherent pronouncements of well-meaning but muddle-headed enthusiasts. Moreover, while a good deal of lip-service is often paid to the value of aesthetic education, it tends to remain largely neglected and underrated.

Indeed, the question is to be taken seriously of whether aesthetic education *is* a logical possibility and not a contradiction in terms – as would seem to be the view of a number of people, including some in positions of power as far as education is concerned. Or perhaps it is that, however sympathetic they might be in principle, they are not very impressed by much of what goes on in schools and colleges under such headings as 'the aesthetic and creative', or by its 'rationale' and the inflated and sometimes pretentious claims so often found in the literature of the subject. A case for aesthetic education is apt not so much to be overstated as understated, since the character of the undertaking is regularly misrepresented. Not everyone who is critical or sceptical about this area, therefore, is to be dismissed as a philistine or perhaps an insensitive, hard-nosed economist.

Unless, then, we are prepared to address ourselves to the question (to couch it in its traditional terms), 'How are aesthetic judgements to be justified?' and produce not a glib or pat answer when challenged, but one capable of being demonstrated in practice, and unless learners themselves are put in the way of understanding the procedures involved, we shall be vulnerable to the charge that we are not engaged in education at all. Either pupils will be left merely to 'do their own thing', with little knowledge of or care for standards, or what goes on will amount to a kind of indoctrination or at best an unwitting transmission of personal or group preferences and prejudices.

One way in which problematic concepts are often illuminated is by comparing and contrasting various uses of the term in question within everyday language with various uses of closely related terms. But the value of such a procedure is sometimes limited, and in the case of the aesthetic is practically nil. Perhaps Scruton was exaggerating somewhat when he claimed that the aesthetic is altogether 'absent from our common thought' (1974, p. 17); but despite what appears to be a rather wider currency of the term today, especially within educational discourse, he was right that there is no ordinary concept of the aesthetic. For, originating as it did from a special coinage of the eighteenth-century German philosopher, Alexander Baumgarten, 'aesthetic' remains primarily a technical or semi-technical concept featuring within philosophical discourse. It is here, therefore, that it is best understood; and it is to attempts to achieve a better such understanding, along with similar attempts in the case of art, that I now turn.

# 2

# *How Is the Aesthetic Related to Art?*

Before investigating the concept of the aesthetic by looking at its relationship with art, we may find it useful to note the term 'aesthetics'. This is usually understood as referring to a type of theoretical inquiry – philosophical, psychological or sociological, as the case may be – as distinct from the aesthetic mode of awareness with which such inquiry deals. But sometimes this distinction is blurred and 'aesthetics' is used where it would be more accurate to speak of aesthetic awareness (or experience, interest, appraisal, etc.), rather as 'ethics' can be ambiguous as between the study of ethical behaviour, attitudes, standards, principles, etc., and those attitudes, standards, etc., themselves. Conversely, 'aesthetic' is sometimes used to denote theoretical inquiry, especially in respect of art, as when someone speaks of Collingwood's aesthetic, meaning Collingwood's theory of art. There is also, outside philosophy, that popular, rather vague use of both 'aesthetic' and 'aesthetics' to indicate a set of unsystematized beliefs held by an individual or group about a particular art form or art in general, rather as 'philosophy' is often used in a rather loose sense, as in the expressions 'his philosophy of education' or 'her philosophy of life'.

Less confusing perhaps, but an error none the less, is the identifying of philosophical aesthetics with philosophy of art. For aesthetics, at least in principle, deals with matters other than art, although in practice many philosophers today tend to be almost exclusively concerned with the arts and art criticism, so that aesthetics becomes a sort of meta-criticism – inquiry into the nature and grounds of critical appraisal and evaluation of artworks. The relationship between philosophy of art and art criticism is, however, one of some complexity (see Scruton, 1983, ch. 1).

Second, it is of some importance to note that the concept of the aesthetic evolved during the eighteenth century from the *ethical* concept of disinterestedness – opposed, that is, to that of self-interest. The idea gradually emerged that some thing or activity could be appreciated not only for its functional efficiency or its craftsmanship, as morally uplifting or theoretically interesting – that is, as serving some purpose – but as a possible source of intrinsic satisfaction, something to be prized for its own sake. A lake, for instance, in contrast to (though perhaps as well as) being valued as a means of water supply for a city, a place for sailing or where children might play, and so on, might be enjoyed for, say, its shape and proportions, its changes of colour, light and shade, the sombre or tranquil or menacing quality of its appearance under various conditions.

Now during the last two hundred years or so, this interest in something for its own sake has been a dominant feature of the Western idea of art. Certainly a work might also be of interest from, for example, an economic, religious, moral, psychological or political point of view. But in the main it has been denied that it is valued as art if it is valued only in terms of such categories of understanding. For this is to treat it as something more like, for instance, a sermon, a clinical remedy, or a piece of propaganda; or as merely a functionally well constructed object or skilful performance. If, then, someone were to regard music simply as something useful to march to or to promote supermarket sales, he would hardly be concerned with it from an artistic standpoint; similarly in the case of a performer if he were to engage in drawing, acting, dancing, singing, etc., merely to display technical ability, or to obtain emotional relief, or for the opportunities for social contacts afforded by the activity.

Yet before the eighteenth century the suggestion that songs, pieces of sculpture, plays, dances and so forth were to be valued apart from any social, moral or religious function they served, or on account of the skill displayed in relation to some particular purpose, would have been all but incomprehensible. Perhaps an aesthetic interest might now be seen as having lain dormant over the centuries, finding articulation only gradually – though from time to time, as in Plato's *Ion* and Aristotle's *Poetics*, there seem to be hints of a groping towards a view of art as an independent, autonomous mode of experience (see Schaper, 1968). But the conception of art as something to be appraised in its own terms, enjoyed for its own sake, was in the main unfamiliar to classical antiquity, the Middle Ages and the Renaissance alike.

Indeed, in the classical era, the Greek term *techne* and its Latin equivalent *ars* extended to a host of products and activities which included not only some of those now typically classed as fine arts (such as sculpture), but also to what are now usually regarded as crafts (such as carpentry), as well as to theoretical disciplines, such as the physical sciences, logic and certain branches of mathematics. Such activities were seen as involving knowledge of a kind capable of precise formulation in terms of rules or principles: art was that which could be achieved according to a blueprint or formula – and hence capable, it is important to note, of being straightforwardly learned and taught. The much later view of art as something to be valued over and above its usefulness or any theoretical interest it served – and hence *not* capable of being learned or taught directly – was therefore nothing less than revolutionary.

Similarly, the concept of beauty had no particular connection with art before the eighteenth century. In classical times, for example, it was most consistently applied to the moral good – to human conduct and character. The notion of the aesthetic, on the other hand, *is* rooted in that of the beautiful, although the word invented by Baumgarten was an adaptation of the Greek *aesthenesai*, meaning 'to perceive'. Hence his book *Aesthetica* (1750) might have been expected to treat of perception. But instead it amounted to a theory of art and beauty based on the thesis that beauty is a property of things when perceived as wholes, and that this perception yielded knowledge of a special kind, unlike that involved in ordinary perception (which issues in claims that such and such is the case). Aesthetic perception, Baumgarten thought, constituted a sort of in-between mode of understanding, inferior to rational cognition yet more than mere sensory awareness. Certain other philosophers of the period who belonged to the British empirical tradition, however, regarded beauty and ugliness as features requiring for their perception the exercise of a special mental faculty, the faculty of 'taste' (known by some as an 'inner sense'), which was supposed to function in a way analogous to that of the 'external' senses.

It is thus possible to see in the work of those philosophers who preceded Immanuel Kant (generally acknowledged as the 'father' of modern aesthetics, though his achievements here also represent the summation of the work of Baumgarten and other Continental as well as British philosophers) an early intimation of one of the most keenly contested issues in the subject and one with obvious significance for education – namely, the epistemological status of the aesthetic. And since *aesthenesai* has further connotations to do with direct awareness of feeling and emotion, a connection between aesthetic appraisal and the affective response of the individual was also indicated.

For a considerable time, however, aesthetic experience was discussed as frequently in relation to nature as to art. But eventually, via the idea that the fine arts (*les beaux arts*) sought to imitate what was beautiful in nature, an association came about that was thereafter taken for granted until approximately the end of the nineteenth century.

This conception of an artwork as a thing of beauty reached its peak with the 'art for art's sake' movement which flourished during the latter part of that century, especially in the fields of literature and the visual arts (Johnson, 1969). Whatever further interest a work might have, it was held, was irrelevant to its status as art. In its most extreme form, this doctrine of aestheticism demanded that art not only need not but must not have any concern other than beauty. Such a view thus goes beyond the claim that aesthetic interest is a necessary feature of artistic interest. Furthermore, the movement was typically associated with a special attitude towards life as a whole – also known as aestheticism: art and beauty were regarded as supreme values, even sometimes to the point of all others being despised.

Small wonder then that when the fashion for adopting various extravagant forms of behaviour and dress was set by

Oscar Wilde, one of its most brilliant, self-parodying devotees, the notions of art and the aesthetic became identified in the popular mind with aesthetes and aestheticism – an identification that has had unfortunate consequences, not least in education, where it still seems to linger on (cf. the reference to 'overtones of dilettantism' in *Curriculum 11–16*, already mentioned). Small wonder also, however, that early in this century a reaction set in among artists and their public alike – although a turning to the hideous and the grotesque, the harsh and the discordant, etc., is sometimes misunderstood (as in the APU document) as a rejection of an aesthetic standpoint. Rather, it is but the reverse side of the same coin.

However, far from remaining restricted to the idea of awareness of beauty or ugliness, whether in respect of natural phenomena or art, aesthetic experience had already in the eighteenth century come to be conceived of as extending to a far larger range of qualities. So while experience of beauty or ugliness is a sufficient condition of aesthetic appreciation (that is, if someone regards something as beautiful or ugly, then he is appraising it aesthetically), it is not a necessary condition (that is, for an appraisal to count as aesthetic it does not *have* to involve beauty or ugliness). And we need to look a little more closely at how some of the ideas about the aesthetic have changed and developed over the years before we can pursue further its relationship with the concept of art.

Now the supposition that beauty and ugliness are properties residing in things – indeed, that there are any sorts of properties at all that somehow exist independently of the human mind – had been challenged by Kant (in his *Critique of Pure Reason*) before the end of the eighteenth century. Our sense perceptions are not merely visual, auditory, etc., impressions, but involve a measure of interpretation, though some are so basic to our grasp of reality that we scarcely realize they *are* interpretations (a 'size-blind' person, for instance, would not share with everyone else the experience of a single objective world). But aesthetic qualities, Kant further argued (in the *Critique of Judgement*), are to be thought of as constituted in a way which contrasts with that of ordinary, everyday perception – one in which our powers of imagination and feeling function differently.

## HOW IS THE AESTHETIC RELATED TO ART?

On this view, now quite widely accepted in broad outline but with some variations of detail, there are no distinctively aesthetic features such as beauty or ugliness that are perceivable and recognizable as are, say, loudness, hardness or angularity. Rather, an object of ordinary perception is regarded from a special standpoint ('under a particular description', in contemporary philosophical language); and this involves a certain freedom of judgement and discrimination, an active personal response that has a markedly affective, as well as intellectual, dimension.

This is to claim that the aesthetic mode of appraisal has an ineliminably subjective and evaluative character. But it is not subjective in the sense that the object of interest is 'all in the mind', as in the case of dreams or hallucinations; nor is it a matter of merely personal preference, as with liking or disliking certain food or drink or bodily sensations. If indeed this were the case, aesthetic experience would be more in the nature of a passive reaction caused by things. Moreover, it does not follow that because an affective response is involved aesthetic appraisals lack objectivity in the sense that they are not open to rational justification. This will be considered in more detail in Chapter 4. Three points about the idea of an aesthetic *attitude* or *mode of attention*, however, may be noted at this stage.

First, it follows from the view that aesthetic awareness is a matter of how we attend, rather than what we attend to, that in principle anything can become an object of such awareness (and hence is possible in connection with any curriculum activity). This is perhaps a somewhat difficult suggestion to entertain initially, but it might be pointed out once again that an aesthetic appraisal can be *un*favourable, yet still be aesthetic; and, further, that in attempting a philosophical analysis we are concerned with formal requirements. Moreover, it does not mean that in practice everything is equally aesthetically arresting.

Second, since on an 'attitude' account there are no distinctively aesthetic qualities or concepts, *any* word or phrase can function aesthetically in the discussion of works of art or other objects of aesthetic interest – not only that handful consisting of 'beautiful', 'pretty', 'ugly', 'unsightly', and the like, which normally do function primarily, if not exclusively, in this way.

Indeed, a host of concepts from other disciplines, as well as from everyday talk in connection with, for example, the life of feeling, characteristically feature in aesthetic discourse (cf. Schaper, 1968, on 'aesthetic transposition'). If, then, we speak of the organic growth or frenzied quality of an artwork, say, this is intelligible because such terms are understood first and foremost in some other field; but they gain a new significance when applied in the aesthetic situation. It is thus the particular context that determines whether a concept is being used aesthetically or not (and in education it is vital that pupils become thoroughly familiar with this usage and accustom themselves to using a wide range of terms and expressions that are appropriate to whatever is under discussion).

Third, if aesthetic qualities (to use the term as shorthand for what, on attitude accounts, is expressed more accurately as 'qualities viewed aesthetically') were of the sort that admit of verification procedures similar to those suitable in the case of colour, shape, size, etc., the aesthetic would be a species of fact-stating or informative discourse rather than a contrasting mode of experience altogether (cf. Meager, 1970).

However, there continues to be some measure of support for theories which, in contrast to attitude theories, characterize aesthetic interest in terms of the perception of what are claimed to be aesthetic, as distinct from non-aesthetic, qualities – most notably in recent decades by M. C. Beardsley (1958), F. N. Sibley (1965) and I. C. Hungerland (1972). Such accounts are therefore sometimes known, if somewhat confusingly, not only as 'perception' but as 'objectivist' theories. Something *is*, for example, graceful as a thing *is*, for example, red; but it is a different kind of quality. How the contrast is to be drawn and what is the nature of the relationship between aesthetic and non-aesthetic qualities may vary as between one version of this type of theory and another, but typically there is reference to the need for specially perceptive or discriminating observers (or listeners or readers) in the case of what are claimed to be aesthetic qualities, while no such special powers are required in the case of non-aesthetic qualities. On this view, then, aesthetic education is chiefly a matter of training individuals in a particular kind of skilful perception, bringing them to discern certain qualities that are not straightforwardly observable, but yet *are* observable.

Such theories have incurred the criticism that they fail to do justice to the importance of the experiencing subject's response and come near to reducing aesthetic awareness to a branch of ordinary perceptual awareness. For it seems that even if an aesthetic quality is widely valued, someone who did not value that quality could nevertheless perceive it (Sibley, 1974): it is a case of his picking out such qualities, of recognizing rather than responding to them. Moreover, it is difficult to see how on this sort of account concepts other than those belonging to the 'beautiful'/'ugly' group come to have an aesthetic usage (Scruton, 1974, ch. 3).

Some kind of attitude theory therefore seems more securely grounded than a perception account, though this does not mean that we must abandon all talk of 'aesthetic perception'. For the term need not imply treating an artwork, say, as a map (to borrow Elliott's analogy) on which we search for objective features. As with the term 'aesthetic quality' or 'aesthetic object', 'aesthetic perception' may be understood as indicating a *way* of regarding things (or events, activities, performances, etc.). Nevertheless, Elliott (1972) may well be right that its widespread use, rather than 'aesthetic experience', is symptomatic of a tendency to consider the arts as forms of inquiry (precisely the expression used in *The Arts in Schools*, para. 7c).

Exactly how an aesthetic standpoint or attitude is to be characterized is, as might be expected, a matter of perennial debate. However, pending fuller discussion in Chapter 4, it may be said that aesthetic awareness involves an imaginative apprehension of some object encountered at first hand, whose form thus perceived yields a certain satisfaction or dissatisfaction: interest is in something regarded *as if* it existed purely for being looked at, or listened to, or (as in the case of literature) in some other way imaginatively contemplated. 'Contemplation', it might be suggested, is another term in aesthetics that is best understood as having a technical, or perhaps semi-technical use; and it may extend therefore, in my view, to the case of someone, say, carving a piece of wood or playing a recorder. Anyone so engaged is certainly, and in a most important way, also an observer or listener, and might be taking an aesthetic interest in what he is doing. Nevertheless, we could not understand what it would be to engage in aesthetic activity unless we could understand what it would be to enjoy contemplating objects (in the sense I have just indicated).

In contrast, then, to the individual's more usual preoccupations with activities simply as means to ends, aesthetic interest involves his being in some sense *detached* from his everyday concerns; in the language of some aesthetic theories he is engaged in an act of *disinterested* contemplation. This notion of disinterestedness is thus related to its ethical forerunner in as much as the experience in question requires that a person is liberated from the need or desire to devote all his energies to satisfying personal desires and appetites – from the demands of what Iris Murdoch calls 'the greedy organism of the self' (1970, p. 65). Hence it is out of reach of those who are not in a position or have not yet learned to overcome such demands, as in the case of the very young.

Yet are not children taking an interest somewhat akin to an aesthetic interest, it might be asked, when they gaze entranced at the glistening patterns of frost on the window pane, or at the darting to and fro of exotically coloured fish in an aquarium? What of their evident pleasure in daubing with paint, or in chanting or listening to jingles, rhymes and other rhythmically ordered sounds and words; in telling or listening to stories, in dressing up and entering the world of make-believe, in apparently purposeless movement such as repetitive stamping, waving their arms about and hopping from one foot to another, as in the manner of a primitive dance? Certainly such activities might seem to be *for their own sake*. Yet they might not be a manifestation of *aesthetic* interest: they might be more in the nature of fantasy play than an exercise of imagination, or prompted by curiosity or the desire to show off; or the enjoyment in question might be of a purely sensuous kind.

How anyone is to know when another individual *is* aesthetically involved – especially when, for instance, he simply 'stands and stares' – is obviously no easy matter, though it is of vital importance in education. Nevertheless, unlike the gambolling and frisking of other young animals, for example, some of the activities just mentioned can fairly readily be developed beyond merely random outbursts of movement or sound – can be selected and refined, especially with appropriate encouragement and guidance from a knowledgeable adult. And attempts to impose a certain order on what at first is probably a source of mainly sensuous pleasure would seem to be connected with that capacity traditionally held to be fundamental to the aesthetic mode of awareness, the capacity to delight in *form*.

Many questions remain to be examined. For example, the claim that aesthetic interest is to be contrasted with practical, moral and theoretical interests, that there is no concern with matters beyond the object or activity itself, raises doubts about its relationship to the serious business of living. Aesthetic and artistic activities might seem to be a luxury, harmless enough but unimportant, in education even a waste of time. We might also wonder about what marks out aesthetic imagination from, for instance, the sort of imaginative attention Newton paid to falling apples; what more precisely can be meant by 'form' in the context of aesthetics, by 'the object itself' and 'for its own sake'; how aesthetic satisfaction and dissatisfaction are to be distinguished from other sorts of satisfaction and dissatisfaction; and, in the case of literature, what could count as an object of ordinary perception.

Not least in need of further clarification is the concept of disinterested contemplation, which has often been the focus of a good deal of adverse, if sometimes misdirected, criticism (see, for example, Cohen, 1965; Charlton, 1972). Indeed, the whole idea of an aesthetic mode of attention has been called into question (see, in particular, Dickie, 1969). Often, however, it is not so much the intelligibility of the concept that has been the subject of controversy as the relevance of aesthetic qualities to the appreciation of art – in particular to literature. For to contrast aesthetic awareness with our more usual concerns might seem to suggest that if it is central to art there is a radical divorce between art and the ordinary world. Yet it is a common experience, and one that might be thought important in education, that a good many art works enlarge and illumine our understanding of all sorts of issues – social, moral, political, psychological, etc.

However, talk of a gap between art and life may involve confusion of a conceptual question with a practical problem –

the problem, as Richard Wollheim puts it, of 'the many different devices . . . by which art has been segregated from those for whom it was made and turned into the preserve of the rich and the arrogant' (1973, p. 335). It is also important not to confuse a *philosophical* account of the aesthetic with *experiential* considerations: to distinguish is not necessarily to separate, and to claim that there is a logically distinct mode of awareness does not mean that, in actual experience, it is always cut off from other modes. Aesthetic interest may be, indeed would often seem to be, part of a more complex totality of experience. Thus a work of art, a piece of furniture, a plot of land, might simultaneously occasion a variety of responses: aesthetic, historical, commercial, and so on. In J. O. Urmson's term, our interest may be 'multiply-grounded' (1962, paras 7, 8 and 9).

Again, the view that for something to be appreciated as art it must be regarded aesthetically does not entail that only qualities of, say, elegance, liveliness or unity are of importance in appraising a work. The issue of whether a particular painting or film, or whatever it might be, is either less or more valuable on account of such qualities than for the subject-matter with which it deals – a matter for *critical judgement* – must not be mistaken for the *philosophical* question of whether art and the aesthetic are logically related. Nevertheless, it might be mentioned here, in advance of further consideration of the point in later chapters, that any interest of a social or psychological kind (for example) that a work may have cannot be wholly separated from the structured form – from that particular configuration of images, rhythms, colours, etc.

A discussion about the relative importance of a work's subject-matter and, say, its economy or expressive vitality presupposes, however, that such qualities are of *some* concern, even if only minimal in a particular case. In other words, a logical connection between art and the aesthetic is not being denied here and might even be taken for granted by those in conversation. But to claim that something lacked aesthetic interest altogether, yet was nevertheless a work of art, would be to rule out such a connection: to question in effect the well established view summed up by P. F. Strawson that 'it would be self-contradictory to speak of judging something *as a work of art* but not from the aesthetic point of view' (1974, p. 183).

## HOW IS THE AESTHETIC RELATED TO ART?

This traditional position is invariably shared by philosophers with a particular interest in education. Louis Arnaud Reid, for example, states quite firmly that 'when one is talking about the arts seriously, the focus upon the aesthetic aspect of art . . . is *logically* necessary if the talk is really to be about art' (1969, p. 18). And, although P. H. Hirst speaks in the main about the arts and seems more interested in the possibility of 'literature and the fine arts' constituting a distinctive form of knowledge, he just as readily refers to 'the aesthetic mode of experience' (see various papers in his collection *Knowledge and the Curriculum*); and in *The Logic of Education* (we may assume it is Hirst speaking) he says, 'enjoying the arts is impossible without concepts that make aesthetic experience available' (p. 62).

The orthodox view of the relationship between the aesthetic and art, however, has come to be challenged, though more often because of a concern that the concept of *art* may not best be understood if it is seen as logically tied to that of the aesthetic than because of concern that the concept of the *aesthetic* may not best be understood if its central cases are taken to be works of art. One reason for this challenge on the part of some (for example, Binkley, 1976 and 1978) has been an interest in so-called Post-Modern art. There have, of course, been 'anti-beautiful' movements in the arts since the beginning of the century. But a direct assault on the whole conception of art works as objects of aesthetic contemplation was launched in the 1960s by a group of painters in the United States, and subsequently by artists elsewhere in a variety of spheres, whose 'items' or 'pieces', as they preferred to call their exhibits, sought to overthrow the assumption that an art object is a work of imagination, and that it requires in turn a 'distanced' contemplator who is expected to make an imaginative response to something tacitly assumed to be an *image* or *fiction* or *illusion*, a carefully constructed composition capable of more than one interpretation, constituting as it were a world in itself.

Contrary, then, to the suggestion sometimes made that what such artists were trying to do when, for example, they exhibited such things as ordinary household articles, holes in the ground, or everyday movements and noises (sometimes contributed at random by the audience) was to stimulate aesthetic contemplation of what is not usually attended to in this way, the intention rather was that these objects, activities, events and happenings, when labelled 'art', should *not* call forth an aesthetic response. Often they invited 'creative' intervention; what was presented was to be used, altered, added to, perhaps even consumed or destroyed.

Now some people might say that before trying to get others to question their ideas and beliefs about art some of these artists should subject their own to scrutiny, especially perhaps their preconceptions about *aesthetic* appreciation. And certainly it is rather naïve to suppose that quietly looking at or listening to something is necessarily to be uninvolved (as many teachers will be aware); or that, conversely, moving about and making a noise is necessarily to be engaged in an activity, let alone in a creative enterprise. (This is not, of course, to say that an apathetic audience might not be provoked into a more lively, thoughtful response by being required to participate in novel ways.)

It is also tempting to object immediately that the items and 'performances' in question simply are not art, and that those who bestow such a title upon them are not artists at all but frivolous devotees of the trivial, the repetitious and the boring, who merely want to draw attention to themselves and see how far they can go in shocking and duping a gullible public or members of the art establishment. Yet while there will probably always be charlatans who will try to jump on to what they see as a rolling bandwagon, and some motivated purely by the prospect of economic gain, it ill becomes the educated lay person, much less anyone with responsibility for educating others, to dismiss peremptorily whatever does not conform to what he has always taken for granted as acceptable in art (or anything else). Certainly a good deal of rubbish has been paraded in recent years under the banner of 'art', as well as considerable nonsense talked about it, but all this can occur too in the case of works of a more traditional kind. Moreover, it has almost always been those who have already earned the title 'artist' as a result of successfully working along established lines who in any generation have made significant leaps forward in enriching the concept of art or of a particular art form.

What the more sophisticated post-modern artists were doing and saying therefore deserves at least a hearing. For one of their chief aims was to question the very concept of art and much else that is generally accepted within the world of fine arts. Many of the problems they pose either implicitly or explicitly are, in fact, philosophical – about meaning, perception, reality, representation, imagination, etc. But, instead of discussion within a philosophical text or a novel or a play, the item itself is the problem: we are confronted with something that teases, maybe baffles our understanding as to what it *is*. Was this pile of sand put there by an artist or a bricklayer? Is that a real flag, a painted flag, or a painting *of* a flag? In other words, is the object or event really art or merely a chunk of everyday reality?

In some cases the intention may be precisely to deny that there is any such distinction; the claim is that the object or movements or sounds (or absence of sound) are simply what they are. But this is to beg a number of vital questions. What is left unclear – as, indeed, with the idea of enjoying something for its own sake or appraising something in its own terms – is how the *it* in question is to be understood. For the 'same' thing can be seen from a variety of points of view. Nelson Goodman, discussing the question of imitation, puts the point succinctly: 'The object before me is a man, a swarm of atoms, a complex of cells, a fiddler, a friend, a fool, and much more. If none of these constitutes the object it is, what else might? If all are ways the object is, then none is *the* way the object is' (1968, p. 8).

If, for example, we are to look at a painting simply as a canvas covered with oils, we might well ask with Arthur Danto: 'What makes us want to call *art* what by common consent is reality?' (1973, p. 4). Either there *is* a difference or, if art succeeds in completely obliterating it (and throughout the twentieth century the history of painting in particular can be seen as a series of moves in that direction), it is, as Danto says, just another way of arriving at something we already have. Art must then cease to exist. Indeed, Ruby Meager (1974) sees the situation as a kind of death of art, art driven to suicide. Far from being available to many, it becomes the preserve of a few highly specialized artists and art critics.

Needless to say, a reaction has already set in. Moreover, it might be pointed out that simply because something 'comments' on art it does not follow that it is itself an instance of art. Various things may feature importantly within the history of art, yet not themselves be artistically significant (Dickie, 1976; Diffey, 1979). Nevertheless, items such as Andy Warhol's *Brillo* boxes and John Cage's *4'33"* – not to mention Marcel Duchamp's ready-mades of a much earlier period – seem to have won recognition as art (and it is far less common for something acclaimed as art to be demoted to non-art status than vice versa, though it may, of course, fall out of favour from time to time).

Strawson's thesis, then, that the notion of the aesthetic is to be clarified via the notion of art, since the two are in his view logically coupled, immediately runs into difficulty if account is taken of the many revolutionary developments in the various arts during this century, especially the latter half. Such a procedure, it might be thought, is founded on too narrow a conception of art. There would seem to be problems too for Wollheim's view, powerfully argued in *Art and Its Objects*, that aesthetic experience is possible only within a society possessing a concept of art – that aesthetic appreciation is an extension of an attitude to be understood primarily by reference to art works. Yet, even if we restrict discussion to art works that predate the post-modern movement, Wollheim's argument may not be convincing.

Richard Beardsmore, for example, suggests that it is possible to imagine a society whose members 'are untouched by any form of artistic activity and yet still possess a love of nature which one might call aesthetic . . . because this is to some extent true of children in our own society' (1973, p. 364). Such a possibility tends to be obscured, he thinks, if we conceive of aesthetic contemplation of natural phenomena chiefly in terms of such things as landscapes and sunsets (often associated with art). What children find enchanting in nature, on the other hand, is not so much what is serene and magnificent as what is odd, grotesque, or bizarre: monstrous jellyfish, 'the curious spectacle of a silver disc suspended in the sky which changes in shape from night to night and which disappears in the daytime', even, perhaps, cows and pigs.

Now such things *may* be enjoyed aesthetically by children (as well as by adults), but the question arises once again of how we are to tell whether such 'enchantment' is *aesthetic* rather than to do with, say, intellectual curiosity or a kind of awe or even horror. Yet Beardsmore would seem to be right in insisting that there are aspects of the appreciation of nature that cannot be understood on the basis of artistic appreciation. Those who argue against this may have forgotten, he says, 'what it was like to be a child looking at a toadstool'. (I shall return to this aspect of the problem in Chapter 6.) He is in no doubt, however, that it does not do justice to the complexity of artistic appreciation to suppose that it is simply one variety of a mode of awareness explicable on the basis of an awareness of natural beauty. Our response to a play, for instance, is not just a more complicated or sophisticated version of our response to, say, a rose. Beardsmore's conclusion therefore is that the concepts of art and the aesthetic, though having strong contingent connections, are best thought of as logically independent (leaving us, however, without further elucidation of how, more precisely, each is to be characterized). If he is correct, it follows that aesthetic education and education in the arts are also to be conceived of as similarly independent, though with important links.

Nevertheless, even if the claim is false that art works constitute paradigm or central cases of the aesthetic, and necessarily involve an aesthetic standpoint, it can hardly be denied that a great many are valuable sources of aesthetic experience (as this has so far been sketched). And many more, perhaps the majority, continue to be produced under the concept of the aesthetic (even if the artist is unaware of what, logically, this involves) and can appropriately be appraised only by adopting an aesthetic approach, whatever developments take place on the fringes. For the purposes of the remainder of this book, therefore, I shall refer to art exclusively in these terms. In any case, innovation and revolution, whether in art or other spheres, can be understood only against the background of what is already familiar and has previously been established and recognized. Post-modern art, for instance, is intelligible only if one is acquainted with works that presuppose an aesthetic stance, and to some extent also with art theory and art history; perhaps some grasp of certain philosophical issues is also required. This, of course, is likely to be beyond the scope of most pupils in schools, though a study of twentieth-century art would hardly be complete without some reference to what anti-aesthetic artists have been exercised about and trying to achieve.

Moreover, much of what many adults think of as revolutionary in art is already a good deal older than they are themselves, let alone their children and grandchildren. As with scientific and technological developments, what may seem strange and incomprehensible to parents (and some teachers) is often readily acceptable, interesting and exciting to young people. This applies also to certain well established art forms and genres. String quartets and operas, for example, often thought of as highbrow and somewhat esoteric, appear to be gaining in popularity among younger age groups – perhaps as a result of television and of interest in pop music featuring small groups, in musicals such as *Evita*, and in works specially for children, such as Britten's *Let's Make an Opera* and *Noye's Fludde*. What is undeniably important in education is that an open-minded, receptive attitude be cultivated towards developments in the arts (no less than in other spheres), while at the same time an unthinking readiness to run after every new thing simply because it *is* new, at the expense of neglecting works of value from the past, be discouraged.

If, however, some pupils reach the stage when they can profitably consider anti-aesthetic pieces of art, it is questionable whether, as part of a general education, they could be expected to produce – or 'find' – such items themselves. For, in addition to a grasp of the conceptual issues involved in thought *about* art, such attempts demand considerable maturity and experience if they are to have any chance of succeeding – a measure of wit, a sense of irony, paradox, and the like which will be found only, if at all, among a few gifted individuals who are already well 'inside' the discipline of art.

By contrast, aesthetic experience both within and outside the arts is possible in the primary school, even if sometimes at a rather lowly level. As indicated earlier, a basis for aesthetic development in art would seem to be offered by young children's liking of rhythmic and patterned play activities, stories and songs, of joke-telling, riddle-posing, mimicking and games of 'Let's pretend', and such like. Whether what they themselves produce can be dignified by the title 'art', however, and whether there is such a phenomenon as 'child art', are questions that can be tackled only by a more detailed inquiry into the concept of art.

# 3

# *The Concept of Art*

There can be little doubt that for some time now ideas about art have been in an exceptionally fluid state. Of course, questions about the merits of a particular piece are always with us, and for the very good reason, as I shall discuss in the next chapter, that there can be no fixed criteria of excellence to which all works conform. But during the present century a more fundamental problem has become acute, namely, what is to count as art. A question that has long engaged the attention of philosophers – ever since, that is, the notion of fine art replaced that of the arts as crafts – has thus become a subject of more general interest and one clearly of importance in education: What is art?

Yet it is not only such things as Robert Rauschenberg's bed or Carl André's firebricks that give us pause for thought, but also, say, ice-dancing, ornamental gardens, birdsong, objects found on the beach or fellside (*objets trouvés*), radio and television plays that seem to be something between fiction and documentary, and a host of other items, including the products of children's endeavours in so-called creative writing, drama, dance, etc.

Questions of the 'What is . . . ?' variety, however, are often not susceptible of a ready solution or an immediately concise answer. To ask about the nature of art – or of related concepts such as literature, music, architecture, or tragedy, beauty, rhythm or form – in the expectation of receiving a brief, compact answer that adequately covers all cases yet rules out 'illegitimate' contenders is to be unaware of the pitfalls involved in attempting to define such concepts. There are, nevertheless, plenty of short, snappy 'definitions' to hand:

'Art is expression', '... the representation of reality', '... the creation of forms symbolic of human feeling', etc.; as well as pithy statements about the supposed function of art, such as that it expresses the imagination or promotes the brotherhood of man, which is then set up as *the* defining feature of art.

Now such formulae are typically highly condensed summaries of complex theses worked out by philosophers of art or by critics or artists themselves, though in every case later shown to have some serious flaw. Yet such theses and the context in which they were originally developed, together with the problem of how the key terms featuring within the would-be definition are themselves to be understood, often tend to be ignored. It is sometimes overlooked, for example, that Wordsworth's well-known dictum about poetry, 'the spontaneous overflow of powerful feelings', which is often extended to art in general, is followed in one place (In the Preface to the *Lyrical Ballads*) by 'It takes its origin from emotion recollected in tranquillity' and in another by 'and though this be true, Poems to which any value can be attached were never produced... but by a man, who, being possessed of more than usual organic sensibility, had also thought long and deeply'. In any case, artists themselves, while sometimes providing valuable insights into their own works – perhaps too into a particular art form – are no better equipped *as* artists than anyone else who lacks training of the sort required for high-level generalization.

On the other hand, claims such as that art is the construction of forms may be emphasizing an important part of the truth about art, or at any rate a good deal of art, and serve as timely reminders of what may be in danger at a particular period of being overlooked or undervalued. Indeed, placed in their historical context, overarching theories of art will almost always be found to have arisen at a time when thought about art, or developments within the arts themselves, have been seen as moving too far into one direction and in need of a push the other way, or else redirected along another track altogether.

Sometimes, attempts to challenge a view of art prevailing in one era have issued in a formula which might be regarded as a slogan for a new way of, say, looking at paintings, as in the case of Clive Bell's 'art is significant form'; in other words, what C.

L. Stevenson called (in an excellent essay first published in 1938) a *persuasive* definition – one that attaches a particular meaning to a word whose use tends to change over time but which retains strongly emotive overtones (the 'true' or 'real' or 'proper' meaning, it is claimed – terms that should always alert us in this connection). Such words, Stevenson points out, are always concerned with something that is regarded of major importance in human life, such as 'culture', 'freedom', 'beauty', which (like 'art') are 'prizes which each man seeks to bestow on the qualities of his own choice' (1963, p. 35).

Since approximately the middle of this century, however, theory construction on a grand scale based on some allegedly defining feature of art has fallen into disrepute in philosophical debate. The demand 'Define your terms', which typically implies a request for a verbal equivalent whereby some quality or set of qualities is singled out as common to all instances of the concept, has become widely regarded as one to be rejected. To ask for necessary and sufficient conditions, it is commonly argued, is to fail to recognize the sort of concept art is – namely, one which it is not merely *as it happens* difficult to distinguish in this way, but *logically impossible*. Any answer could be only so general or so trivial or contentious as to be of no value (see, for example, Weitz, 1978).

Indeed, art is a classic instance of what W. B. Gallie has suggested are 'essentially complex and essentially contested' concepts (1964, ch. 8) – concepts that are in general use but lack satisfactory elucidation. Like history, democracy and Christian doctrine, for instance (Hartnett and Naish, 1976, argue that education be added to the list), the concept of art is not only as a matter of fact regularly contested, but of its very nature contestable. Yet this, Gallie maintains, is no disadvantage: such concepts involve something that is highly valued, and the impossibility of pinning down their meaning exactly keeps these subjects constantly in the forefront of debate.

One procedure recommended by many philosophers in place of attempts to define (for example) 'art' – often associated with the 'ordinary language' approach – is the adopting of the 'family resemblances' model made famous by Ludwig Wittgenstein (though a very similar notion was suggested by a Scottish philosopher, Dugald Stewart, as long ago as 1810

(Osborne, 1968; Diffey, 1973). That is, as in the case of games (Wittgenstein's example), we are likely to find that instances of art, rather than sharing a distinctive property or set of properties, form a family whose members are related by strands of similarities, 'and a whole series of them at that', this one here connecting with that one there, that one with another, but not any one with all (*Philosophical Investigations*, para. 312). (In trying to find out about a thing or a person we do indeed often ask what that individual is *like*.)

However, such a scheme has never been worked out in detail in respect of art. In any case, the suggestion involves various difficulties. For example, is it not necessary to know first of all what constitutes the 'family'? With, say, the Churchills or the Mountbattens it is possible to detect likenesses of a brow here, a mouth or eyes there, and so on, since we already know who counts as a member (should someone who had no biological kinship chance to have a similar feature or features, this would not be a *family* resemblance). But in the case of art this is just the problem: what we are seeking to establish is which candidates are or are not instances of the concept.

To this it might be replied that the way to proceed is to pick out samples of what seem indisputably to be works of art – as one might, for example, try to work out whether something is to count as a game by starting with cricket, marbles, hopscotch, etc.) and then look for significant similarities in the case of the new claimant. Now certainly any satisfactory account of art has to accommodate those instances of which it could reasonably be said 'Well, if *that* is not art, what is?' Yet we should not suppose that even if the enormous task were ever achieved of establishing the major likenesses between such paradigms we should then have a complete set of resemblances to which we could always thereafter refer in order to determine what else belongs to the category of art. For each newcomer, once admitted, could itself provide the basis of further comparisons.

Another important question that arises in connection with the family resemblances model – as well as with many definitional accounts of art – is what *sort* of features are in question here. And in more recent years attention has been focused on the importance not of ordinarily observable properties of objects, nor yet of qualities such as expressiveness, but rather of the nature of the relationship between the activity of the artist and the responses of the public, on the place art occupies in the life of society, that is, on *non*-exhibited characteristics. Someone, then (to take an example from Danto), looking at a painting and protesting that all he can see is a white oblong with a black line across it cannot be helped to see it as art by examining it more closely. For it is not, as Danto remarks, as if he had overlooked something; 'and it would be absurd to suppose he had, that there was something tiny we could point to and he, peering closely, say, "So it is! A work of art after all!"'. What is needed rather is 'an atmosphere of artistic theory, a knowledge of the history of art: an artworld' (1978, p. 140).

This notion of an artworld has proved somewhat difficult to specify. How, for instance, are its members to be identified? Might there not be a literary artworld, a music artworld, and so on? Nevertheless, the germ of Danto's thesis (to some extent foreshadowed by Gallie), namely, that art has to be understood as a social and historical phenomenon involving an intricate web of activities and practices – exhibiting and performing, discussing and reviewing, learning and teaching, etc. – is of the utmost importance (not least for education). Further attempts to shed light on the concept of art have therefore tended to centre on this 'institutional' character. There has even been a return to the attempt to define 'art', namely, in terms of an artefact having the status 'candidate for appreciation' conferred on it by someone 'acting on behalf of the artworld' (Dickie, 1971, 1974, 1976).

What has increasingly been recognized as vital for an understanding of art is that how we 'take' objects (using this term to cover performances, events, activities, situations, etc.) depends on their history and on what is known or assumed about the particular context (or 'atmosphere') surrounding them – an insight we owe largely to Wittgenstein. Art, in a famous phrase of his, is a 'form of life': we can appreciate something as art only as a result of being on the inside of 'a whole culture', 'the whole environment' (1966, p. 8). Just as the handing over of a set of homework or money for school meals, for instance, requires an understanding of a network of assumptions and beliefs that are normally taken for granted in a community, rather than made explicit, so with art. One learns what it is, what counts as an art work, chiefly as a result of belonging to a society in which certain activities are carried on and certain traditions followed – typically in places specifically designed for the purpose, such as theatres and galleries; in special centres of training and study, such as studios, conservatories and colleges; by means of journals, auctions, festivals, and so forth.

A basis for such understanding is thus usually laid at a relatively early age, since a good deal about these practices is mostly picked up in the first place quite casually – absorbed, one might say – from what, for example, goes on in the home (especially since the advent of radio and television) and from visits to the theatre, the cinema and the park, with its bandstand, pieces of sculpture, etc. In other words, from seeing people looking at and listening to and reading certain things, and perhaps talking about them – as well as, of course, by having them described and explained from time to time. This understanding is likely to be reinforced and enlarged at school – and not only in periods devoted to children's own artistic (or quasi-artistic) activities, but also through events such as exhibitions and concerts which mirror, if on a smaller scale, aspects of the larger (art)world. Indeed, to examine the ways in which a child begins to acquire an idea of art aptly illustrates the merit of Wittgenstein's suggestion that in attempting to understand any concept we might try to recall how the relevant word or words are typically learned – for instance, 'art', 'work of art', 'poetry', 'fade-out', 'etching', 'sonata'. Similarly with various artistic conventions: the child, like Flute the bellows-mender, has to learn that not all the words on the printed page, 'cues and all', are to be spoken as part of a play.

Of course, from time to time certain practices and conventions undergo change, both in terms of what is created and produced in the name of art, and how it is presented. For example, instead of actors moving about on a stage addressing one another, they may be immobilized in urns or a mound of sand and talk to no one in particular; performances of poetry, music, dance, etc., may take place in factories, public houses or the street; new genres such as kinetic art and jazz ballet may develop, as well as new combinations of previously existing art forms; even new art forms may evolve such as, in this century, radio and cinematic arts. But, whatever the changes and innovations, in order for a new item to gain art status it has to be possible for at least some people – typically the more artistically educated – to make relevant connections between that item and what has previously been accepted. It comes to be seen as capable of being placed within the 'collection' of what already counts as art. And it is precisely when it seems that *every* convention is being broken, as for instance when railway timetables are strung together and called a poem, that widespread doubt may arise as to how this can be regarded as art – or even, as in this case, poetry.

What ultimately counts as art, then, is not something determined by a flip of a coin or a decision on the part of a single individual, even if he has reflected conscientiously on the question. It is no more a personal matter than is, say, science or morality, but requires a measure of general acceptance, though how much and by whom is part of the problem.

It follows from the view that art is an institutional matter and not (if anything is) a 'brute fact' that a piece of wood or a sequence of movements, say, may be art in one society or during one era but not in another. Everything depends on the interlock of attitudes, beliefs and values of the community in question, the kind of esteem accorded to various objects and achievements. Hence what were once venerated as religious objects in one society, or used for military or agricultural purposes, etc., might in a different setting, another social or temporal context, be regarded as fine art (consider, for example, the contents of the pyramids or certain ritual dances). Thus it is too that a claim to art status has sometimes been made on behalf of quite ordinary objects: had they been left on a kitchen shelf or a beach, untitled and unmentioned in any catalogue, the claims could not even have been made, let alone stand any chance of being successful.

The arts, however, not only reflect but are partly constitutive of the culture within which they develop. Far from being a merely decorative crust, they help to mould its thinking and sensibilities no less than, say its political and educational institutions do. Indeed, some sociologists (for example, Foster, 1976) have suggested that, even if the artist may not be a revolutionary in the sense of trying to effect rapid social or political change, it is he who gets at the root of our behaviour, changing our perceptions and perhaps eroding certain ways of thought and feeling. Hence it is hardly surprising that totalitarian governments keep a close watch on what artists – and critics – do and say. On the other hand, in capitalist societies the arts may become commercialized to the extent that they are trivialized and rendered innocuous.

Not every member of a community (in the West) plays an equally active part in its artistic life, of course, or is aware of being affected by the arts. For, in addition to difficulties of access such as financial and social barriers, certain art works may also be inaccessible in as much as some, perhaps many, people lack the necessary education to be able to take advantage of what is on offer. Such individuals are therefore particularly liable to be baffled when radical changes occur. Yet it is not so much that they have *no* concept of art; rather, it is a limited concept. Remarks such as 'Call *that* art?' when, for instance, sculptures 'full of holes' or constructed of string or old tyres are exhibited, indicate that, although the speaker may (at first, at any rate) refuse to accept a particular work as art, he nevertheless does have an idea of art. They also further illustrate the inescapably *evaluative* nature of the concept: what is acknowledged as art – or as sculpture, music, etc. – has to come up to certain expectations.

Most people probably can in fact point to a considerable number of examples of art: they can give, that is, an ostensive definition. To ask what art is, then, seems to be asking a question to which the questioner himself can already supply some sort of answer, even though he may not be able – and usually is not able – to give an adequate account of the concept. Yet 'art' is not exceptional in this respect, for we operate successfully with a good many concepts that are not easily analysable, and can understand and use correctly all sorts of words we may not be able to define. One has only to think of children here, of course. But it does not follow that such concepts cannot be both expanded and refined; and art is one that can continue to develop throughout life rather than be acquired once and for all. Somewhat paradoxically, therefore, the greater someone's experience of art, the more hesitant he might be in applying the term in a particular case: his use of 'art', and perhaps especially 'work of art', is highly evaluative (cf. Diffey, 1973). (Whether *any* term is free of evaluative overtones is a matter of controversy in contemporary philosophy, however.)

An educator, then, has simultaneously to widen the learner's concept of art and help him become more discriminating, more critically aware. Similarly, what is needed when someone is inclined to reject out of hand what has more recently become accepted as art is the assistance of another person with greater understanding of the arts than he possesses and who is able to find some connection or series of connections between the object of puzzlement and what is already appreciated as art by the individual concerned. For the richer a person's experience of art, the more likely he is to be able to identify innovations *as* innovations, to place new items in some sort of historical perspective, to set them against the background of both established and less well known works.

A lively-minded lover of the arts may, indeed, actually hope to have his expectations upset from time to time, whereas someone more conservative may get held up at some point in the development of a particular art form – with, say, Georgian poetry or Romantic classical ballet. Yet it can also happen that individuals of limited experience – including, sometimes, children – may bring to a comparatively unknown item a freshness and lack of strongly developed preferences that allow them to respond enthusiastically, even though they may miss many of its subtleties and be unaware of the precise nature of the artist's achievement.

Whether, however, children's own efforts are to be counted as art is no easy question. On the one hand, while their products may have been widely displayed within a school, such recognition alone scarcely seems sufficient to set the seal on the precise status of whatever is in question. Yet, like unpublished manuscripts or scores, but quite *un*like 'works' which an artist might claim to have 'in his head', children's products have the *potential* to rank as art, or at least embryonic art, in as much as they are, in principle at least, publicly accessible.

Moreover, they are importantly different from natural phenomena such as shells or the singing of birds or whales, or even the paintings of Betsy the chimpanzee at Baltimore zoo which have been exhibited in an art gallery. For artistic activity involves certain beliefs and assumptions on the part of an agent as regards what he is doing – and these are embedded in a social setting where similar beliefs and assumptions are crucial to his intentions and expectations. Thus, although someone who did not know that some coloured marks on paper had been made by a chimpanzee might suppose them to be the work of an artist, just as he might also take a piece of rock for a sculpture by Barbara Hepworth, for example, his responses are likely to be significantly different when he learns otherwise. However outwardly similar to some natural object an art work might be, it is not a *natural* phenomenon, but the outcome of thoughtful activity. Even when accidents, chance happenings and the like are used, they are typically worked on or into the final form; likewise *objets trouvés*, minimal art, and so forth, require certain intentions and decisions as regards their public presentation. Hence the possibility in art of outstanding or mediocre or flawed achievement.

An artist, therefore, cannot merely indulge his personal whims; for what he puts forward for public scrutiny presupposes its being regarded as the result of certain choices he makes within a limited range of options and possibilities. These possibilities, however, are at the same time constraints, brought about on the one hand by the medium and the material(s) with which he works and, on the other, by the techniques, styles and images that are already familiar to him. His achievements thus involve an ability not merely to handle tools or control limbs and vocal organs, etc., but also, typically, to recognize and seize on specifically musical or kinetic or visual or literary challenges and problems as these present themselves at a certain time in art history. To work within a certain medium is to do more than work with a set of materials; it is to employ those materials with some measure of how they have already been used for artistic purposes. Any artist, no less than a scientist, stands (as Newton put it) on the shoulders of giants: he inherits, though without always fully realizing this, certain assumptions about his medium.

An art work, then, is both created and appreciated as art not as an isolated phenomenon but against the background of other artistic achievements. Hence in the artist's selecting, discarding, refining and ordering of what he does there is always a critical element. By contrast, nothing of this happens as far as we can tell – or could tell in the absence of a common language – in the case of animals. Despite, for example, what seems to be the deliberate organizing of sounds by birds, whales, dolphins, etc., we cannot know precisely what significance this has for them. It is we who hear the result as a sort of singing, we who may find their movements and other 'performances' of aesthetic interest. (For that matter, this is possible even with marks and sounds that come about unintentionally, as in the case of footprints or the notes struck by the proverbial kitten on the piano keys.) Indeed, we could not attribute artistic ability to an animal, whatever was produced; for, even if there were anything in its world amounting to traditions such as are essential to our conception of art, they would be outside our comprehension. As Wittgenstein vividly expresses the point, 'If a lion could speak, we could not understand him' (1953, p. 223e); neither language nor art is separable from the tissue of knowledge, beliefs, customs and values which each springs from, yet also articulates.

If, therefore, to take a related example, we stand before a spider's web, admiring its delicate texture and intricate structure, and murmur 'It's a work of art!', we cannot mean literally what we say; rather, this is a way of expressing that admiration. For in front of what we know *is* an art work this is the sort of remark we should hardly be likely to make: only in exceptional circumstances could it have any point. Furthermore, it is significant that while we might quite properly speak of sounds, marks and movements produced by animals as beautiful, lovely, graceful, etc., or as joyous, melancholy, plaintive and the like (qualities that are expressive for *us*), it would be quite out of place to refer to them as, say, witty, pompous, perceptive glib, exalted or pedestrian. Such ascriptions, commonly found in critical discourse about art, indicate that the concept of art as we have it is normative: it involves the notion of standards.

Neither would such terms normally be applied to what young children produce. Moreover, if an individual is unable, or for some reason unwilling, to talk about, for example, a picture he is looking at or has painted, there are difficulties similar to those that arise in the case of animals for anyone who seeks to ascertain the nature of that individual's experience. Nevertheless, while it cannot be certain that, for instance, an apparent show of pleasure in a product or activity is a manifestation of *aesthetic* satisfaction, there are other ways in which such satisfaction may be shown by a child that are not typical of birds, monkeys, and so on. For, in addition to persisting with what are recognizable as *efforts* with clay, movement, a musical instrument, etc., regularly repeating or modifying the result, he may be making these adjustments as a consequence (or so it would seem) of watching or listening to what others do in similar circumstances, or noticing how they respond to his endeavours or those of others, including their own. In other words, he may show signs of learning; and when children consistently manifest some interest in such responses there is a good chance that they are beginning to develop some measure of artistic awareness.

It is when a child has some command of language, however – a difference between humans and other animals of paramount importance – that it becomes possible to be more certain whether he *is* acquiring a concept of art. For now he is able to make specific references to his own and other people's products and performances, to pay more attention to relevant (and, if only roughly, nameable) qualities and features of poems, plays, dances and so forth, and to indicate that he shares appropriate beliefs about and attitudes towards them. For example, he can show by questions and remarks, as well as by other kinds of behaviour, that he appreciates that pictures displayed on the classroom wall are (typically) to be looked at for sheer enjoyment, whereas objects, say, on the nature table, though also able to be admired for their colours, shapes, structures, etc., are more usually examined from the point of view of 'What is it?', 'Why is it like that?', 'Where did it come from?', and such like. Children further come to understand that certain standards are applicable which lead people to say such things as 'Do you think those colours or these go together best here?', 'The beginning was interesting, but can you make the ending more exciting?', 'Notice the difference when we pause at this point', 'What about that big space over there – are you going to leave it quite empty?'

Finally, what of the notion of 'child art'? A troublesome concept, as M. K. Diblasio (1983) argues: first because it is ambiguous, indicating sometimes the products of a vaguely defined age range, sometimes a putative style; and, second, because it is an ideological construct (though not recognized as such by those who employ it), based on ideas such as the natural unfolding of innate powers of creativity. It seems originally to have come into prominence in connection with drawing and painting towards the end of the nineteenth century, when many artists came to value spontaneity and even a certain *naïveté* and crudeness, and saw in children's efforts qualities they themselves sought to emulate. And in education, though at a later date, and for a variety of reasons, such ideas spread to other arts; ideas about naturalness, freedom of expression and the unfettered play of the imagination took precedence over regard for precision, careful ordering and the faithful representation of things.

Now for the sophisticated adult children's products may well seem artless and unaffected (taken literally, these terms are indeed significant). But once again this is possible only when they are viewed in the light of the observer's richer knowledge and experience of the arts. Such qualities are not intentionally achieved by a child as they might, on the contrary, be striven for by a mature artist; and they do not constitute a *style* any more than one's fingerprints are a stylistic matter. The envious adult is thus likely to be suffering from what Ernst Gombrich (1960) has powerfully argued is 'the myth of the innocent eye' (quite uncritically subscribed to by Herbert Read, for instance). Any suggestion that there could be a *natural* artistic style or a kind of art independent of any tradition is wholly incoherent. Paradoxical though it might at first seem, originality and freshness of vision are possible only when there is some grasp of what has gone before. There could thus no more be child art than there could be child chemistry, child history or child arithmetic. All too often children's early movement play, explorations with crayons, percussion instruments, and the like, are theorized about in such a way as to fit some overall theory of a dubious nature about education, human development and, indeed, about art, which is damaging to all. Such activities might more accurately be characterized in sensory-motor terms or as both an attempt to find out about the world and an indication of how that world is perceived.

This is not to deny that older children of primary age and into the early years of secondary schooling (it is impossible to be exact here) do often reveal in their artistic endeavours a spontaneity and readiness to experiment and innovate which, given appropriate encouragement and critical response, may be retained along with the development of other important qualities. But what they (and especially young children) do can hardly rank as art while it remains unrelated to intentions and beliefs of the kind discussed here, and unconnected with some measure of thoughtful reflection. Art may well be an essentially contested concept, but if its application is extended to anything and everything that goes on in schools in the name of 'creative activities' we shall have lost our grip on it altogether.

# 4

# *Imagination, Feeling and Aesthetic Education*

Aesthetic awareness, it was claimed in Chapter 2, consists in the adopting of a particular attitude or standpoint which involves discrimination and judgement on the part of the experiencing individual. It is not a matter of his recognizing certain features of things in the way that he discerns their size, shape, solidity, colour, etc. Rather, his imaginative powers are actively engaged in a special way such that his perception of, and with that his response to, an object (or event, activity, performance, and so on) has a significantly affective dimension.

Moreover, aesthetic appraisal is immediate – which does not mean that it necessarily occurs spontaneously or without reflection, but that it is unmediated, not inferred. In seeing a child as pretty or hearing a piece of music as exuberant, for example, one does not ascribe these qualities to the child or the music as a result of theoretical reasoning, adding up various observable items and working one's way to a logical conclusion. One simply sees the prettiness, hears the exuberance; or in the case of literature is directly aware of, say, the relaxed pace of a novel, the subtle complexity of a poem. And in experiencing such qualities the aesthetically involved person is intimately caught up with the object, whereas perceiving that it is long or large or high-pitched or square might be a matter of complete indifference to him.

How, then, are aesthetic responses capable of modification? How can there be less or more refined discrimination? Can there not be improvement, development, progress in one's aesthetic endeavours, whether as a spectator, a listener or a reader, on the one hand, or, on the other, when for instance choosing clothes, making or arranging something, or when performing a song, a dance, a role in a play? In other words, how is aesthetic education possible?

To try to answer these questions – implicit within aesthetic inquiry ever since it first evolved – it is necessary to look more closely at the idea of imaginative attention and its relationship with ordinary perception, together with the idea of taking pleasure in something for its own sake, and, since these inevitably bring us up against knowledge claims, at the problem of the objectivity of aesthetic appraisals.

## Imagining and Perceiving

A great variety of performances and activities falls under the heading of 'imagination', ranging from the forming of mental images (seeing or hearing 'in one's mind', *in* imagination or what I shall call 'imaging') to exploring possibilities or entertaining thoughts about what might be, what might have happened if . . . (what I shall call 'supposing'); from certain kinds of 'seeing (or hearing) as' to doing something imaginatively, *with* imagination (cf. Furlong, 1961; Redfern, 1982, Essay A). Even if the concept can be established as a unitary concept, characterized perhaps in terms of a contrast with what is actually the case, it is essential in order to understand more fully the distinctive nature of *aesthetic* imagining to consider various kinds of imaginative experience and how they are linked conceptually to perceiving, sensing, believing, thinking and feeling.

We may begin with the contrast between aesthetic and ordinary (or normal or literal) perception, with the reminder that for an aesthetic stance to be possible at all there must be available to ordinary perception some object with features of the kind which can be checked by standard tests for truth – what are sometimes called 'first-order' features. Unless, for example, one can see the lines and curves of the stone wall of the Chapter House of Southwell Minster, one cannot see its carvings as having, in Nikolaus Pevsner's words, 'a noble and vigorous stride, youthful yet stately', its leaves 'fresh and resilient, lustily spreading over all the capitals' (1945, p. 11).

In this respect, therefore, the aesthetic situation is unlike that which involves *imaging* – as in the case of a child who 'sees' monsters and the like coming through the bedroom walls during the hours of darkness, or of another who actively conjures up images of such monsters. There are, of course, important differences between the two. The first is not an agent, but a passive sufferer in the grip of false beliefs; the second, who voluntarily *forms* images, is under no such delusions, not a prey to fancies or 'mere imaginings'. But in neither instance is there a sensory object which could be brought to someone else's notice. Hence we cannot directly share our mental images, whether of the sort over which we have no control or those we deliberately call up.

In aesthetic perception, on the other hand, since there *is* something with publicly observable features to which another person's attention can be directed, there is the possibility that he too will see, as we might, the unity or imbalance of an art work, say, or the gaiety or sombreness of a classroom's décor. We do not, of course, always notice every straightforwardly perceptible detail just as, when we see an individual as depressed or cheerful, we are not always aware of, for example, his drooping shoulders or sparkling eyes and suchlike. Nevertheless, it is just that particular configuration of lines, gestures, words, notes, etc., in a particular context that makes it possible for something to be seen as having qualities such as gracefulness or an elegant finish. It is not that the first-order features explain the gracefulness or whatever it might be: they constitute it. As Meager puts it: 'You can't be beautiful as you are without having a certain shape, colour and size, and you are beautiful as you are in virtue of these and not simply in addition to them' (1970, p. 308).

However, although aesthetic perception is logically dependent on ordinary perception, this relationship is not one of entailment. That is, it does not follow from the fact that something has first-order features a, b, c . . . n that it must on that account be either beautiful or ugly (for example). Hence the need for judgement in such appraisals, not the application of ready-made criteria.

Now, what were referred to above as 'straightforwardly discernible' details are not equally obvious to everyone. It might, of course, be objected that nothing is straightforwardly discernible, since (as mentioned in Chapter 2) all perceptions are more than mere sense impressions, involving as they do some measure of interpretation. Nevertheless, there are some features that are more straightforwardly observable than others and for which there are standard tests, applicable in standard conditions by standard observers – as in the case of colours. Yet there still might seem to be a difference between perceiving, say, dark colours or straight lines and, by contrast, chromatic scales or Doric columns. This, however, is simply a matter of acquiring more sophisticated sortal (or classifying) concepts. Once someone possesses the concept 'chromatic scale', for example, he is thereafter (in normal circumstances) capable of recognizing (note, re-*cognizing*) particular instances of that concept. For here there are well defined criteria of identity. Hence he cannot come to hear it as, say, a major scale or an arpeggio.

Although we might refuse to *look* at or *listen* to something, once we do we are not free in ordinary perception to *see* or *hear* what we know to be this or that as some other thing. To perceive correctly is to take something for whatever it is. Of course, we may make a mistake, either on account of some physiological or psychological disorder or because of certain perceptual conditions. If, for example, the light is poor, we might mistake (*mis*-take) a tree for a person. But with improved conditions such errors can be corrected: true belief replaces false belief and we are no longer able to take it as we did before.

It is possible, however, to recapture the earlier experience by an act of imagination. Although we now know the true state of affairs, we might deliberately go beyond that knowledge and once again 'see' the tree as a person, that is, we *see as* in a different, though related, sense. Similarly where there is no previous perceptual error. In this sort of imagining, then, when we experience something differently from how we know it actually to be, we have a measure of freedom that is not possible in ordinary perception. There are, it is true, certain constraints, some in respect of the experiencing individual (such as his knowledge, sensibilities and cultural background), others in respect of the object and the context in which it is set (a river, for instance, could hardly be seen as a pin). But whereas, normally, seeing (or hearing) is believing, believing is *not* involved in *experiencing as*.

We continue, of course, to hold beliefs about the object of ordinary perception. And in the case of aesthetic imagination, which is a kind of 'experiencing as', it may be important for an appropriate response whether someone believes that what he is looking at is, say, a carving, or whether he takes it to be a piece of driftwood found on the beach. But beliefs about an *imagined* object are, as it were, resisted. Thus one might see a carving as full of force and rhythmic energy, while knowing perfectly well that the wood is no longer alive and growing. It is not that concepts such as 'vigorous' and 'lively' are applied incorrectly in such a case, for the concern here is not with expressing beliefs. Rather, concepts are used in a way that reveals a response which depends precisely on an awareness of this freedom from belief. Far from there being, as Coleridge put it, 'a willing suspension of disbelief', perceiving imaginatively necessarily involves disbelieving – though certainly willingly (that is, freely).

Now like ordinary perception, *thinking* too typically involves believing. But again there is an important exception, which is marked by the features of voluntariness and freedom from belief just discussed, and which assists an understanding of imagination (admirably set out by Scruton, 1974 and 1979, to whose account this sketch is much indebted). This is the sort which consists in entertaining a thought while not accepting it as true. Scientists, for example, as well as historians and philosophers, often 'play' with an idea in attempting to throw light on a practical or theoretical problem, while nevertheless aware that such a thought might be false, even that it *is* false. Yet this kind of thinking – imaginative thinking – is essentially rational, for it takes off, so to speak, from an understanding of what *is* the case, and involves no confounding of reality and unreality, as in delusions and hallucinations. Similarly with aesthetic imagining – though here 'make-believe' is engaged in not for some further purpose but for its own sake. Moreover, as with the framing of a scientific hypothesis, a distinction is to be drawn between the wildly fanciful or fantastic and genuinely imaginative activity: the thought has to be appropriate to that on which it is focused and retains an important link with awareness of reality. (This will be discussed again later.)

It might be mentioned here that, since aesthetic experience is a species of imaginative attention and does not involve belief therefore, it is sometimes said to be 'non-cognitive' in character. This might be a source of some confusion within the context of educational discourse where, in common with everyday discourse, 'cognition' is apt to be used in respect of *any* kind of thinking, though the suggestion that aesthetic understanding is to be contrasted with propositional knowledge, or 'knowledge-that' (which does, of course, necessitate belief), often finds ready acceptance among those concerned with aesthetic education. But to claim that aesthetic awareness is non-cognitive does not mean that it requires no intellectual effort, even if this is apt to vary in degree according to the object or performance in question. Nor is it to deny the possible importance for aesthetic appreciation of knowledge one might *bring to* the situation, as indicated in the previous chapter.

To ask someone to use his imagination, then, can carry a number of different meanings. It might, for instance, be an 'order' to call up a mental image, as in 'Imagine a dog with three heads'. Alternatively, it might be to do with seeing coals in the fire as faces or hearing the sound of the wind as voices. Or it might be an invitation to think about – to entertain the possibility of – what it might be like to be prime minister or what might have happened if Japan had won the Second World War.

The fact that all these sorts of suggestion can be acted upon is of considerable significance for education in a number of fields; and to understand how *aesthetic* education is (logically) possible we have to take account of the capacities human beings have both to 'experience as' and to entertain a thought while not believing it. Such invitations as those just mentioned might sometimes prove difficult in particular cases, but they are both intelligible and reasonable, whereas it makes no sense to tell someone to have a *sensation* such as travel sickness, to like or dislike a certain scent or flavour or texture, or actually to see or hear something (though in all these cases he might be able to do something else first in an attempt to bring about such results). Moreover, an individual can be helped to achieve imaginative experiences of the 'seeing (or hearing) as' kind not only by direct suggestion such as 'Can you see a desert scene in these tea-leaves?' but also by having his attention drawn to certain first-order details or to certain relations between them that he had previously missed. 'Look,' we might say, tracing or pointing to various shapes and arrangements of the leaves (coals in the fire, clouds, etc.), 'there is the camel, there the men, the trees . . .', and with that he may come to see as we do. Similarly, the other person – even a child – might bring further details or different relations to *our* notice, so modifying our original perception or even altering it altogether.

In the aesthetic situation, clearly, the more experienced an individual is in paying close attention to details and ways in which they may be seen as interlocking with one another, the richer his imaginative experience is likely to be. This might be expected to be especially the case in the arts. For typically the artist has intentionally included and woven together, as it were, just those particular details – an inversion of a musical or visual motif, a juxtaposing of sound and sense as in 'killed'/'cold', 'crow-black, sloe-black, slow, black' etc. – in just that particular way. There are also all sorts of conventions in the arts knowledge of which may enable an individual to perceive more easily than he otherwise might what there is to be perceived (for example, the giving of a title to a piece; programme or catalogue notes).

But we have not yet established what makes for distinctively *aesthetic* imagination; and as the next step we might consider further the 'experiencing-as' situation where, as just indicated, it is possible to move not only back and forth between ordinary perception and imaginative perception but from one image to another – in other words, to interpret the object of ordinary perception in another way, rather as, instead of seeing tea-leaves as a desert scene, we might come to see, say, a football field with players, goal-posts, etc. The first-order features remain unaltered, but they are now organized differently in imagination, or maybe rearranged or recombined in respect of just a few details so that the image is only partially, rather than radically, changed.

Thus in aesthetic perception a face might come to be seen not so much as beautiful but as pretty; the opening of Sibelius's Fifth Symphony heard not merely as languorous, but as containing that latent energy which builds up later; Macbeth's 'She should have died hereafter' speech experienced less as a weary sigh of bleak despair than as a cry of bitter rage and frustration. Such changes may be either subtly or dramatically different; and, most importantly in the aesthetic situation, with those changes there is an altered response. We might, for example, be charmed by prettiness whereas we were more deeply impressed by beauty; feel not so much pity for Macbeth at that moment as increasing revulsion. This, however, is not necessarily the case with changes in imaginative perception which is *not* aesthetic (seeing faces in the fire, say); indeed, our affective sensibilities may not be involved here at all. And similarly with imaginative thinking or 'supposing' which is not aesthetic; nor need there by any change of mental image – if, that is, there *were* such an image in the first place.

In the aesthetic mode of awareness, however, imaginative thought, perception and feeling are indivisible. The thought is not, as it might be in other cases of entertaining a proposition without accepting it, a kind of comparing, additional to perceiving; not a conjecture or suggestion that a passage of music or poetry, for example, *resembles* something languorous: we *hear* and not merely think of it as languorous. And that thought/perception is suffused with a response that is not indentifiable separately from the notes or words experienced in just that way. Thus in any change that occurs – if, for example, the languorousness is now heard as charged with a certain rhythmic energy – perception, thought and response are modified together.

When we appraise something aesthetically, then, the experience has a peculiar liveliness comparable with that which is characteristic of imaging. What is in fact absent or non-existent seems vividly present; what we know is not the case nevertheless seems to be so. The languorousness or restraint, the tranquillity or frenzy, comes alive in the colours, lines, movements, notes, words themselves. In this respect aesthetic perception is also somewhat akin to normal perception. Hence it is perhaps hardly surprising that in reporting aesthetic experience we speak typically of the *object*, ascribing qualities to it as if they were first-order properties, and use the same grammatical forms of speech as in ordinary perceptual claims. Just as we might say 'This chair is hard' or 'That bell is shrill', so we might also say 'That's a lovely girl, but she's wearing a hideous hat!' Similarly we say that poems and paintings, etc., *are* poignant, sentimental, well proportioned, and the like. That is, aesthetic remarks resemble straightforward assertions: they appear to convey information, to state what is the case, to have genuinely descriptive force.

This resemblance is indeed significant, for it suggests that the claim is defensible. While the remark is not made independently of the speaker's personal response – how the thing in question affects him – it is nevertheless also in part about that thing (the key term or terms in aesthetic conversation are in fact often adjectives or adjectival phrases, that is, they qualify the object). Yet a not unusual rejoinder might be 'Oh, do you really think so?' or 'Why do you say that?' – queries indicating that the person addressed is not necessarily prepared, at least at first, to agree with the claim; in an important sense, does not understand it. Such queries do not typically arise in connection with claims about chairs being hard or bells being shrill. They would be surprising too if someone said that he had a headache or liked or disliked the grittiness of sand or the sensation of cartwheeling. Any sensible answer here, other than 'I just do', could be only in terms of *causes* – probably of a physiological or psychological nature – not in terms of *reasons* such as are appropriate in the case of claims that something is graceful, grotesque, etc.

## Aesthetic Feeling

Before such reasoning is considered in more detail something further needs to be said about the character of the feeling aspect of aesthetic awareness. I shall use 'feeling' here in a rather broad sense: to define distinctions between moods, emotions and other affective states is notoriously difficult (see Reid, 1970, 1973). 'Pleasure', 'enjoyment', 'satisfaction' (and their opposites) can all be misleading in this context. 'Satisfaction', for instance, might suggest a sense of achievement in attaining a particular goal or the gratifying of some antecedent desire or need; 'pleasure' the occurrence of pleasant sensations – neither of which, I am maintaining, has any part in aesthetic appraisal.

On the other hand, the claim that there is a distinctively aesthetic emotion – a special thrill or sense of transport, say – felt on every occasion by the individual concerned (Bell, 1931) gets us nowhere, though of course one may experience a powerful feeling in the aesthetic situation. But we have only to consider the extraordinarily diverse range of objects, events, etc., that typically prompt aesthetic interest – even just the enormous variety of art works – to realize the implausibility of such an idea; and, if it were then suggested that in each instance of aesthetic appreciation we experienced a particular shade of this putative emotion, we should have to itemize as many shades as there are objects.

Nevertheless, it is only by reference to objects or situations, or, rather, a certain conception (or misconception) of an object or situation, that we can precisely identify our emotions – or, for that matter, any other state of mind: 'an "inner process" ', as Wittgenstein famously put it, 'stands in need of outward criteria' (1953, para. 580). Trying to distinguish mental phenomena as if they were private happenings or states knowable in isolation from things and occurrences in a public world is thus widely regarded as a philosophically suspect procedure. Furthermore, to suppose that experiencing pleasure or displeasure is invariably a matter of having pleasant or unpleasant *sensations* is in effect to accept the old eighteenth-century view that they are never anything but passive reactions over which we have little or no control – a causal view that at best renders aesthetic responses (for example) excusable and in need of explanation, rather than intelligible and capable of justification.

We do not, then, in aesthetic awareness first experience, say, delight or disgust and afterwards look around to find out what is causing it, as perhaps in the case of a sweet smell or a smarting sensation in a finger. Rather, the response (as distinct from a reaction) is rooted in a particular appraisal of something – as delicate, for instance, or ungainly. In contrast to sensations, aesthetic feelings, like other mental states, are directed onto some 'target' – some object (or event, etc.) interpreted in a certain way: in philosophical language, the *intentional object* (from the Latin, *intendere*: to aim). Pleasure and displeasure can therefore be characterized here only in terms of how we 'take' that particular thing, the description under which we see it.

It is thus not beliefs about the perceptual object that change, but our imaginative seeing or hearing. When it is said that something is enjoyed for its own sake the 'it' in question is (in the sense discussed earlier) the imagined object, that which we 'construct', albeit on the basis of something ordinarily perceived. The implied contrast is with interest that involves other considerations – as reflected in, for example, 'for the sake of fame' or 'for the sake of the children'. 'For its own sake' is another way of indicating a lack of concern with the possible uses or purposes of whatever is under review.

This is not to deny that aesthetic awareness might not be affected by additional knowledge or a change of belief about the object of ordinary perception. Learning more about life during the Second Empire of Napoleon III, for instance, might lead us to hear Offenbach's Overture to *Orpheus in the Underworld* not simply as lively and gay, but as frivolous, perhaps rather cynical; what might strike us as a delightful 'ballet' of beautifully shaped objects on the television screen might appear as a sinister, ghoulish performance, a veritable *danse macabre*, when it proves to be a diagrammatic representation of the behaviour of cancer cells.

An account of aesthetic enjoyment which stresses sensory experience, however, might seem to present difficulties in the case of literature, and additional considerations *are* required here, especially perhaps in the case of prose works. True, a poem may occasionally have a certain visual significance, as in Brian Coffey's *Advent*, where the shape of the words on the page is that of, first, a butterfly, then a coffin – the butterfly shorn of its wings; and clearly auditory qualities are often of major importance. But, with the exception of poems where no conventional words are used, the appreciation of literature can never be in sensory terms alone. For it is always in large part dependent on an understanding of the literal meaning of the words and the ways in which words are characteristically organized in a particular language in order to make sense. Thus someone who understands such meanings knows to some extent what a poem (say) is about, and could be expected to offer a paraphrase. But if that were all we should hardly credit him with understanding (that is, appreciating) it *as a poem*; or, if he wrote sentences or phrases that were merely intelligible, with writing *poetry*. Rather, he has to show some awareness of the importance of words and their sounds as specially ordered, of their rhythmic and melodic qualities, of phrasing, balance, and suchlike, all of which make for a further dimension of meaning (contrast, for example, the opening line of Eliot's *The Journey of the Magi*, 'A cold coming we had of it', with 'We had a cold coming . . .'.

Indeed, such awareness might be likened to the kind of 'hearing as' that operates in listening to music, where interpretation depends on experiencing the sounds as grouped in one way rather than another (cf. Scruton, 1983, ch. 6). Even though the enjoyment of many prose works tends to depend rather less on sensory aspects than is the case with much poetry, they nevertheless contribute vitally to, say, the vividness or tautness or turgid character of the writing. Moreover, as Saw insists, an author would not succeed in conveying (for example) moral quality if he were not a good writer (1972, p. 37).

Again, as regards the matter of truth and belief. While much literature conveys insights into human experience, insights that are often some of a work's most important values (as can be the case, however, with other art forms), the object of appreciation is not the sort of thing about which questions of truth or falsity can arise. However 'true to life' it may be it is, to repeat, *imagined*, a *fiction*. Hence the potential danger of speaking, as many educationists do, of 'learning about life' from the arts, as if this were a case of 'learning *that*' (discussed further in the next chapter; cf. also Foreman-Peck, 1983). Far from being creative, artists dealing with life issues (as contrasted with, for instance, purely musical or visual or kinetic themes) would, if tied to factual matters, be restricted like social scientists and others whose job it is to seek out the truth to *reporting* on what is or was actually the case, rather than having a certain freedom to explore possibilities, to show what something is or was *like*, what might be or might have been. Their work would then have to be judged for accuracy of the kind appropriate in the case of documentaries, historical records, etc., rather than subject to criteria appropriate to imaginative constructs.

A further problem traditionally thought to arise in connection with the account of the aesthetic given here as involving pleasure concerns works of art which deal with tragic events and situations. Surely, it is often said, only people who are monsters or perverts could enjoy contemplating the pain and distress of others. But reflection on what it is that is enjoyed in such cases, the intentional object of the response, helps to dispel the puzzlement – such as worries, for example, Diané Collinson in her paper 'Aesthetic education'. For what are contemplated are *imagined* sufferings, even if based on actual events and people. Interest is centred on an artistic creation, on characters (or *personae*); and although we may experience pity, horror, indignation – indeed, a whole range of emotions – they are never raw emotions evoked by raw stimuli. If that were so, we should be either prompted to action – for example, to fly from the scene, set up a disaster fund, and so on – or overcome by nausea, outbursts of weeping, and the like. But whereas in ordinary life we might be anxious for a terrifying report to be over as quickly as possible we often linger over even a harrowing painting, can hardly bear to reach the end of a chilling novel, film or play, and would indeed sit through it all again. Delight is all the time in a *presentation*; nor are we engulfed by fantasy. Thus even Collinson has to admit that she is *glad* to have seen, for example, *Dr Faustus* and Francis Bacon's paintings; whereas, if the events in *Hamlet* had actually happened, she says, 'I would probably spend the rest of my life under the shadow of that experience' (1973, p. 206) (cf. Schaper, 1978; Rosebury, 1979).

This is not to say that the terror, sorrow, pity, etc., that we experience are altogether different from those of everyday life; for in all art, as well as in situations outside art, aesthetic experience is continuous with non-aesthetic experience. Otherwise terms such as 'terrifying', 'anguished' and 'appalling' would have a meaning different in the aesthetic context from their standard meaning – which is clearly not so. This, then, is but another aspect of the thesis that an aesthetic stance presupposes knowledge of what is the case, that aesthetic discourse presupposes factual discourse. But it involves, clearly, another dimension; for in imaginative activity, whether we are engaged as creative artists or performers, as audiences or readers, we are free to *reflect* on catastrophes, absurdities and much else in comparative calm. While we may be deeply involved with a play, a film, or whatever it might be, we are also aesthetically distanced. We may be under a sort of spell as we sit in a theatre or concert hall or stand entranced looking at a stained-glass window or a sunrise, or as we sculpt or sing or act or write or dance. But we are never so completely carried away as to be incapable of breaking that 'spell' should, for example, the building catch fire – rather, it might be added, as children engaged in imaginative play, as distinct from being imprisoned in a fantasy world, are never so absorbed as to be unable to distinguish it from everyday reality (a ruler ready for use as a sword is thus happily loaned temporarily to someone for measuring purposes).

## Form

Consideration of the nature of aesthetic pleasure brings us directly to the question of form as a logical feature of aesthetic awareness. But what is involved here is not so much the actual structure of something in terms of, say, rondo or sonnet form or the proportions of the golden section, as the capacity of the aesthetically engaged person to bring a particular kind of order to whatever he is attending to. In regarding it as 'set apart' from the world of commonplace reality (in the way in which this was discussed earlier), he might be said to *give* something form, integrating it by, as it were, placing it in a frame, at a distance.

Nevertheless, this is often aided, and indeed prompted, by a thing's *actual* structure – if, for example, it is well ordered or organized from a functional point of view, perhaps with almost mathematical precision, either naturally (many shells, horns and plants grow in logarithmic spirals) or in the achieving of a particular aim such as dispatching a ball to a boundary or designing a jug to pour well. Conversely, what is badly ordered may operate against aesthetic interest, though appraisal of something as disorganized, rambling or disjointed might itself (depending on the context) be an aesthetic appraisal. But while, for example, a sweetly timed off-drive or the design of a coffee pot might readily awaken an aesthetic response, the mere fact that the form *is* ideally suited to the purpose is no guarantee that it will merit *aesthetic* admiration. For it is the purposive *quality* that we enjoy when we admire such things aesthetically: we may, indeed, have neither knowledge about nor interest in how they 'work' (hence Kant's phrase 'purposiveness without purpose'; cf. Schaper, 1979, ch. 6, II).

In the case of the arts a great variety of means, both external and internal, assists this formal completeness or set-apartness (*not*, to emphasize the point again, to be confused with 'an emptying of the mind, an isolating of objects in perception, a suspending of all thoughts about them' – Hepburn, 1984, p. 38, in a perceptive essay on art and nature). Externally, as indicated in the previous chapter, there are all sorts of institutionalized practices and conventions, from the very existence of, say, theatres and art galleries to such things as their raised platforms and special lighting. Thus we do not see a painting, labelled and probably framed, etc., as part of the wall on which it hangs – and when in a classroom children 'come out to the front' to act, sing, tell a story and suchlike, this (whether it is realized or not) may, similarly, have the effect of putting an aesthetically significant distance between the performer(s) and those who watch or listen.

Internally, the contrast is typically heightened not only by the way the artist orders sounds, words, gestures, and so on, but also by the artificial character of some of those components – words and phrases perhaps archaic or newly minted, dance gestures that are not just movements that we perform in everyday life. Even the time-honoured opening of many stories, 'Once upon a time', and their endings, 'And so they lived happily ever after' or 'And that's why . . .', serve in part to mark off the artefact – the made form – from what has gone before and what follows: they indicate a departure from and a return to the here and now of ordinary reality.

Most artists, then, seek to evoke and reinforce a 'distanced' response, and to a considerable extent are responsible for the way or ways in which it may justifiably be interpreted. But while a composer or dramatist, say, may work within a traditional form such as classical sonata or one of the sonnet forms, no artist ever conforms exactly to a blueprint or formula. Indeed, this is the very antithesis of what we now usually regard as creative achievement. Although a work often results from assiduous practice in strict adherence to certain rules, it typically involves a flexible use of such compositional forms so that within a particular framework we may nevertheless find surprise and novelty – the felicitous thwarting of certain expectations while others are fulfilled.

To deny that objects of aesthetic interest have form in the sense that they necessarily exhibit, for example, unity or harmony or 'configurational coherence' (Osborne, 1952) is to insist on the uniqueness of the object of aesthetic interest (a logical feature, not a fact established by discovering that all such objects are different from one another). That is, whereas in ordinary perception something is recognized as an instance of a kind, sharing certain attributes with all other members of that kind, to see something as, say, exquisite or hideous is not to see it as belonging to a class of exquisite or hideous objects. There are no such classes, no fixed criteria that mark out exquisiteness, hideousness, etc. Anything experienced aesthetically is exquisite (for example) in its own special fashion – much as we find a person admirable or interesting in a way that no other person is admirable or interesting, but in virtue of just that particular conjunction of attributes that we see as constituting John or Jane (cf. Meager, 1965).

However similar, therefore, to something else a thing might be in respect of its first-order properties or its ability to fulfil a particular purpose, as an object of aesthetic regard it can never be replaced by that other thing. Hence too the need for firsthand acquaintance, a direct personal encounter with whatever is in question. We can never take on absolute trust the report of another person, however knowledgeable or reliable in aesthetic matters he usually proves to be – though this is not, of course, to suggest that there cannot be valuable guides in this realm; hence also the impossibility of being *trained* to make appropriate aesthetic responses or to produce things of aesthetic merit, though again this is not to deny that there are certain skills that might *facilitate* such achievements. Aesthetic appreciation is not an exercise in the detection of a *kind* of quality for which an individual can be schooled in the way that some dogs can be trained to sniff out certain scents; neither can anyone be taught to be creative by advice invariably to adopt certain procedures and avoid others (though provisional 'rules' and constraints might be useful at various stages).

It does not, of course, follow that models and exemplars are out of place in arts education: on the contrary, they may be a most important means of developing aesthetic discrimination.

It may also be useful for practitioner and appreciator alike to cultivate the habit of being on the alert for the possible significance of, say, the interplay of light and shade or the recurrence of particular motifs, images, words, or phrases. But while, for instance, rhythmic variety or intricate patterning might be just what makes for excellence in one context, it might in another prove totally inappropriate. An aesthetic appraisal, that is, holds only for the object in respect of which it is made. Economy, elegance, a subtle transition, etc., can only be *demonstrated* in the particular case – that is, *following* contemplation of a song, a ballet, an Adam fireplace; each one has to be taken on its merits.

There are, then, no universal aesthetic principles or ready-made criteria that can be known in advance and applied automatically – a crucial point on which almost all aesthetic theories are agreed, but one on which the APU document, in its perfectly laudable aim of combating the widespread view that in this realm 'It's all a matter of taste', is apt to be misleading. For it speaks more than once of 'declared objective criteria' and further claims that 'Unless the student has learned the objective criteria of an art form . . . he will be unable to develop his own creative potential' (para. 3.5) – as if there were *sets* in each form to be digested once and for all.

Since, however, this publication also states that one cannot respond appropriately to a work unless one has grasped 'the objective criteria of the concept of art' (para. 3.4v) and talks of 'criteria which is [*sic*] explicitly tangible for all to see' (para. 3.3), as well as artistic meaning being '*to some extent* logically dependent' on certain sorts of context (para. 4.2, my italics), one can only conclude that it was over-hastily put together with no final editing. (This is but a sample of curious remarks – not least in the section headed 'Objective assessment: philosophical foundations'!) This is unfortunate, since among its recommendations for practical assessment there are some well worth considering.

## The Justification of Aesthetic Appraisals

But if there are no standards specifiable in advance, how, it might be asked, can the justification of aesthetic appraisals be a rational procedure? What are we to do if, say, someone finds a film powerfully moving, yet restrained, while another sees it as self-indulgent and apt to 'go over the top'?

Underlying these questions, however, there would seem to be the assumption that reasoning must be of the kind concerned with providing grounds for the truth of a proposition; whereas this, it is now often accepted, is an unduly restricted notion of reasoning. The question 'Why?', asked in respect of an aesthetic appraisal, is to be construed neither as an inquiry of the sort 'What causes you to react as you do?' (that is, requiring explanation), nor yet as one demanding deductive argument (that is, leading from certain premises to a logically clinching conclusion). It is, by contrast, a request for reasons for a response to something, and it is properly answered when the person concerned, employing what Meager (1965) calls 'the ostensive principle', points to certain observable features of whatever is in question in virtue of which he responds as he does. These reasons, however, have to be not only appropriate in his own case but also compelling – though not logically binding – in respect of others as well (not all responses for which there are good reasons are necessarily *justifying* reasons: a child's being upset by the arrival of a new baby in the family, for instance).

This citing of particular details is precisely what is often found in the critical literature of the various arts, crafts, and sometimes in sports journalism: critics and reviewers characteristically provide descriptions of works and performances which may support their interpretations and evaluations. And the successful outcome is that in testing those interpretations against the publicly perceptible features of a play, a necklace, a ski-jump, etc., another person is brought not to believe the truth of a proposition but to share the critic's imaginative perception and, with that, his response. He comes to catch, for example, the sense of fun in Alexander Calder's mobile *The Mulberry Bush*, the 'boiling' quality of the *stretto* of Mendelssohn's Italian Symphony in a performance that saves up something for later on.

Nor is it only professional critics who proceed in this way. Conversations between people at, say, an art gallery or after reading a novel or watching a television play are typically along similar, if perhaps rather cruder, lines. 'What did you think of it?' ('make of it', 'feel about it', as we significantly say), unlike 'Can you pass the salt? and suchlike, is a genuine question requiring a reflective answer. Whatever they may say about aesthetic appreciation being a purely personal matter, few people in fact behave as if they really believe this. Whereas normally there is no sense of obligation to justify a preference for this food or that (the realm where the notion of taste has its natural home), individuals do seem prepared with objects of aesthetic interest, whether cars or carpets or pictures, to try to defend their opinions. Moreover, they often show an interest in those of others and may even attempt to understand appraisals which differ from their own.

Although in practice it may not be easy for someone to articulate his reasons, the underlying presumption seems to be that there *are* justifying reasons, that one's response is not idiosyncratic, but calls for the agreement of others. Discussion may remain at a somewhat desultory level (an indictment of an education that has left so many people almost dumb in the face of some of the things that touch them most nearly in their everyday lives), but it seems to be tacitly recognized that the attempt to justify one's aesthetic responses is in no way absurd. It would, on the other hand, be absurd for someone to try to give reasons such that another might eventually *understand* his culinary tastes or come to share his enjoyment (or dislike) of, say, riding on the Big Dipper as a result of noticing details that the other had previously failed to notice.

The focus, then, in the justifying of an aesthetic appraisal is on the object, not on the physiological or psychological state of the person concerned. Even with attributions such as 'thrilling', 'moving', 'embarrassing', the direction is clearly outward – to something that is open to inspection and discussion. Thus, if someone says of a film, for example, that it was profoundly moving, additional comments of the kind 'It was so evocative of the long, drowsy days of that summer prior to the war, yet had overtones of imminent disaster' themselves stand in need of further elucidation and justification, for they too are of an interpretative character. They just might, on occasion, be enough to enable another person to understand his response (as Sibley suggests in an excellent discussion of how someone may get another to see as he sees – albeit within an objectivist account of the aesthetic – the mere mention of a particular quality may 'do the trick' – 1965, pt II). But, more convincingly, the person making the claim has to refer specifically to publicly observable features of the object or performance, including perhaps technical details. For example, 'Well, the camera work was so skilful in shifting from those long shots of rich pastureland and blue, hazy hills to the family group – close-ups of their gentle, yet rather wistful faces during their leisured conversations . . .'. Often, in practice, the two sorts of remark go hand in hand, and certain information that is not evident from the work itself might also be supplied. To explain, for instance, that ·303 is a machine-gun – the 'you' addressed in Keith Douglas's poem of that title – would be likely to make all the difference to its appreciation if someone lacked this knowledge.

The results in such cases, then, may be that a certain view of the object – a perception (to repeat) imbued with both thought and feeling – becomes clear to the other person. There is a sort of clicking into place so that he too is affected, rather as when he laughs on seeing a joke (cf. Cohen, 1983). But there is no guarantee of success here. In contrast to the situation where one individual takes another step by step through, say, a mathematical theorem, that is, where acceptance of the conclusion can be *demanded* (one and no other), anyone engaged in aesthetic 'argument' or 'proof' can only *hope* that another person will come to share his response. Moreover, he himself might be brought to modify that response as he gives due regard to what the other or others have to say.

Nevertheless, the procedure remains the same, namely, that of referring to yet further details, even those which might at first seem rather trivial, relating them to one another in such a way that an ever fuller and more coherent 'picture' of the thing in question is built up. This referring or 'pointing' is not necessarily or exclusively linguistic, however: one might sing or play a musical phrase, for instance, or gesture or act, in order to convey a particular shade of meaning or draw attention to what seems to be its significance within a larger context. Such a procedure, involving the highlighting and weaving together of relevant details to produce an integrated, convincing account, might itself be considered to have a creative aspect – not wholly unlike an 'account' given by a performing artist, a conductor, a director, and so on, of (say) a dance, a symphony, or a play.

Should profound disagreement persist in spite of even inspired attempts at justification, this can be no less disturbing to those involved than when they fail to agree on a moral issue. We do usually mind if someone rejects our aesthetic appraisal of something, whereas it does not normally matter if, for instance, I like chocolate and you do not. This is hardly surprising; for, unlike our predilections for certain flavours, scents, etc., our aesthetic responses belong inescapably to the realm of values, and as such are not sealed off from all other ideals and interests. Indeed, it would be rather strange if what we found aesthetically delightful or distasteful, humorous or depressing, etc., had nothing to do with what delights, disgusts and touches us in other departments of life. Yet in striving to underline the distinction between the aesthetic and the moral some philosophers are apt to speak as if aesthetic disagreements were of little moment. 'We can live side by side in peace and amity with those whose tastes differ quite radically from our own,' says William Kennick; 'similar differences in moral standards are more serious' (1965, p. 18). This sort of position, it might be suggested, tends to result from taking too little or even no account of aesthetic awareness outside the arts.

We may, indeed, usefully consider the two areas separately in going on to examine further questions in aesthetic education in more detail. But that such a project is possible at all may now be seen as resting on the rational character of that particular kind of imaginative achievement which is a distinguishing mark of aesthetic experience. For such achievement involves, in the first place, an act of will which, though exercised freely, is at the same time subject to certain constraints. In contrast to fantasy (or fancy, as it is sometimes called), which effects a release from the world of reality, aesthetic imagination remains linked with that world in important ways. As John Hospers puts it: 'the imagination, no matter how high it may raise its head into the clouds, keeps its feet firmly on the ground. The fancy, on the other hand, sails into the cerulean with nothing to bind it to the world of common experience' (1946, p. 202). It is not merely that there is an object (or situation, etc.) which the individual concerned is aware exists independently of himself, but that, regarded aesthetically, his understanding of it is transformed. In learning to submit to the controls of a disciplined imagination (whether his own or that of someone else), in contrast to indulging in, say, wildly implausible yarn-spinning, or dramatic improvization or the painting of crudely realistic scenes of violence, or succumbing to the fascination of a horror film or novel, the superficial charms of a dance or a dancer, the surface glitter of flashy clothes, make-up and so forth, he becomes (paradoxically, as it might seem), liberated rather than enslaved by his thoughts and feelings (cf. Scruton, 1983, ch. 10).

Second, that an aesthetic response *is* a response, not some kind of unthinking reaction, is crucial to the concept of aesthetic education. It is not despite but because of its subjective character that aesthetic awareness can be developed and refined. For the feelings involved are rooted in an appraisal of something and can therefore be not only deepened but also modified as a result of reasoned reflection.

To become aesthetically educated, then, an individual has to become progressively concerned both with the aesthetic merits (and demerits) of objects and with the integrity of his own judgements. There is thus a link here with moral education: interest in something for its own sake involves a putting aside of concerns with self-advancement and the gratification of desires and appetites. And since it is only persons – rational beings – who are capable of such interest, to become educated in this sphere is to partake of benefits that are peculiarly human; it is, indeed, to become more fully human.

# 5

# *Aesthetic Education in the Arts*

It follows from the account of the aesthetic mode of experience set out above that aesthetic education consists centrally in the cultivating of an individual's capacity to regard things, including things which he himself might have made or be making or performing, with a particular kind of imaginative attention and to become increasingly discriminating and critically reflective in his responses to them. And since, characteristically, works of art are conspicuous among the things that invite and reward such contemplation (to continue to use this term in the semitechnical sense I have suggested it has in philosophical aesthetics), the arts clearly have a major role to play within the total enterprise.

This is not to say that it is necessarily through art that the foundations of aesthetic interest are laid. Indeed, it would seem likely that a primitive kind of aesthetic awareness is first stimulated when children are introduced to words such as 'lovely', 'beautiful', 'ugly', etc., as their attention is caught by, or directed towards, say, Christmas decorations, party clothes, a firework display, flowers, butterflies, or a person's face or movements. Nevertheless, however sensitive and discerning someone might be in respect of natural beauty, for example, or dress or machinery, he would hardly be considered aesthetically educated if he were unable to respond appropriately to at least some works of art.

In this chapter, then, drawing on the discussion of preceding chapters, I shall examine those questions raised in the Introduction regarding aesthetic education in the arts that have not been considered so far – in particular, questions to do with creativity and appreciation, with notions of expression and communication in the arts, with the education of feeling in this realm, and with aesthetic development and progress in the arts.

## Creativity and Appreciation

It might be suggested that anyone who is aesthetically involved, as I have characterized this, is necessarily creative in as much as he actively 'reconstructs' an object of ordinary perception, and, in responding to the challenge to revise any aesthetic appraisal, not least in re-interpreting a work of art, constantly exercises his creative faculties. Yet since the concept of creativity seems to involve there being some product of quality on the part of the creative person (White, 1972), it might be more accurate to speak of an *imaginative* effort in the case of appreciation. Certainly an eloquent individual may sometimes, in articulating and justifying his aesthetic responses, rise to the heights of producing what is itself a minor poetic gem (consider, for example, Walter Pater on the paintings of Botticelli or Northrop Frye on Eliot's *Four Quartets*). But we are then concerned with some further artefact, and not everyone who finds a work aesthetically arresting is able to produce either a verbal appraisal or some other manifestation of appreciation that is itself of quality.

Participation in the performing arts, however, might reasonably be thought to have a creative aspect, though the decisive part often played here by a teacher in conducting or producing a work (even casting) is often overlooked. So too is the fact that it is possible that a member of a music or dance group may know little more than his own part, and may therefore have far less understanding of the whole than many a spectator or listener. It is, indeed, not unknown for a pupil endeavouring to hold his own line in a part-song to be advised to 'close his ears' to what others are singing; and it seems doubtful whether children in schools are given sufficient opportunity to listen to other interpretations of works which they themselves perform.

There is, of course, a considerable legacy of educational thought and practice which links the arts with practical activity in that restricted sense which the term tends to have in this sphere, that is, leaving their desks and moving about. And this tradition was therefore easily built on when, during the 1930s, the notion of creativity became important, and the 'need' for individuals to pursue their own interests and express their ideas and feelings gained ground. A good deal of such thinking, it may be noted, is rooted in a particular conception of human nature, namely, that everyone possesses an innate creative drive, sometimes identified (as in the case of Read, for instance) with an aesthetic drive; and that this, if allowed to develop naturally, will promote personal and, according to some (again, including Read), social harmony and happiness.

Such a view is therefore often associated with the idea that education involves the provision of an environment in which the child's putative inborn capacity for creativity can be manifested through play, unimpeded by interference from outside. And since the arts are seen as the paradigm of creativity they are to have not merely a special, but a central, place within the total educational scheme. We find echoes of this even today: the Introduction to the Gulbenkian *Report on Dance Education*, for example, states that 'arguably' (no adequate argument, however, is advanced nor the claims of any other subject area considered) the arts 'should lie at the centre of the curriculum' (p. VIII), and mis-quotes (p. 3) the Crowther Report's reference to the arts as 'not flowers, but roots of education' (para. 325): 'not *the* flowers but *the* roots of education' (my italics).

A related idea, also by no means dead, is that (as Read fervently believed) there is a liberating of creative powers in art that is carried over to *all* subjects – a claim which, as we saw earlier in the case of imagination as conceived of in the Gulbenkian Dance Report, suggests a view of creativity as some kind of inner source of mental energy which can either be inhibited or set free to flow into various channels (cf. White, 1972, p. 145). Moreover, since it is further widely assumed that the arts necessarily involve the expression of the artist's feelings, they are often thought of in education as the prime means of healing the alleged division between intellect and emotion – a division made worse, it may further be believed, by the linguistic tradition of Western education and the development of a scientifically and technologically oriented society. Ideas about 'harmonization', however, may vary as between the belief that the (especially non-verbal) arts *integrate* what are regarded as warring aspects of the personality and the belief that they act as 'balancers', providing compensation for academic studies. They may also be seen as pre-eminently useful in the education of children of low academic ability, who, like the 'children of bronze' in Plato's ideal republic, are on this view incapable of rational and abstract thought and had therefore better concentrate on 'aesthetic' pursuits, that is, what are (mistakenly) thought of as involving the sensuous, the physical and the affective, as against the rational, the mental and the intellectual (for example, Bantock, 1971). Also underlying some 'harmonization' theories, there may be the facile assumption that the end of education is happiness.

Although many of these notions are of long standing, they have regularly surfaced in this century in writings on the arts and arts education: to take but one example, in the literature of 'modern educational dance' (for example, Laban, 1963). They also feature prominently in what may have been the first publication to contain in its title (as translated from the German) the term 'aesthetic education', namely, the work of the eighteenth-century dramatist and philosopher Friedrich Schiller, *On the Aesthetic Education of Man* – a treatise that in this country has perhaps had a greater influence on thought about the subject, even if indirectly, than may be generally realized. For in his influential *Education Through Art* Read made considerable use of Schiller's views (or what he took to be his views), particularly in discussing play, freedom of expression and art, and marked him out as one of the two 'witnesses to truth' on education (the other, not surprisingly, being Plato) whom he valued 'more than any others' (p. 284). Indeed, it would seem to be Read who first introduced the term 'aesthetic' into educational discourse, moreover, via talk about *art* – a move which Philip Meeson suggests 'has passed by almost without comment or further examination by art teachers in this country' (1981, p. 180).

In Schiller's hands, however, play is a concept that has little to do with what we normally think of in this connection, least of all children's play, and, if singled out for special attention (as it often seems to be), tends to become separated from his overall theory of the *aesthetic* to the detriment of an adequate understanding of either (cf. Schaper, 1985). Certainly Schiller paints his canvas so widely as to have an instant appeal to anyone caring little for conceptual clarity and inclined to conceive of the aesthetic, along with art, as almost unlimited in scope: both concepts become so stretched as to be practically meaningless. Similarly, Read writes that 'Life itself in its most secret and essential sources is aesthetic' (1943, p. 33). For Schiller himself, art (somewhat like 'the art of movement' for Rudolf Laban) extends to 'the art of living'; and 'artist', not only to craftsmen and artisans of all kinds ('mechanical artists'), as well as, of course, to sculptors, painters, musicians, and so on ('fine artists'), but also to those who shape government and other social institutions ('pedagogic and political artists').

In more recent years a new and even wider concept of creativity has emerged, one no longer derived from and geared to the concept of artistic activity, but extending to spheres of thought and practice, especially science and technology, where inventiveness and ingenuity in relation to problem-solving are involved (Elliott, 1971). This newer concept, therefore, Elliott suggests, may not be so well suited to art as was the traditional concept – indeed, in some ways is antithetical to it. Some enthusiasts for arts education have nevertheless seized on the newer concept, or else jump or slide from one to the other, and so present (or, rather, misrepresent) the arts as a potent means of fostering a capacity for 'creative thought' and 'creative action' on a broad front, a 'quality of capability' (whatever that could be); even, according to the APU document (3.4i), 'a creative approach to life' (whatever that means).

Although, then, the Gulbenkian Foundation's inquiry, *The Arts in Schools*, points out the mistake of thinking here in terms of a general mental capacity (para. 37), it seems to suggest that the arts promote creative development, along with qualities such as intuitiveness and adaptability, in a global fashion; while academic studies, it is implied, do not (paras 2c, 7f). Indeed, the extraordinary claim is made that creativity 'can be developed and trained like any other mode of thinking' (para. 32), which expresses a commitment to the belief that there *are* such general powers or processes. And, again, it sorts oddly with the inquiry's apparent desire (shades of Read once more) to hold up as a model for *all* learning and teaching certain 'principles and methods' the arts are said to 'represent' (paras 3, 43). The assumption seems to be that art-making is largely self-initiated and self-directed, and thus requires freedom from and independence of authority.

If, moreover, as seems to be urged elsewhere in this publication, being creative involves intentionally bringing into being something of originality that is of value as judged by criteria that are appropriate to the particular field in question, it is difficult to see how creativity can be taught at all, let alone trained. It may be, of course, that there are all sorts of knowledge and skills that can be passed on that may be necessary for various kinds of creative achievement, and some methods of teaching may be more conducive to such achievement than others: pupils might, for example, learn the rules of construction for a triolet, say, or a dance in canon form, and have practice in such exercises. But to compose a poem or a dance which has artistic merit requires something more than this. Further, the idea that 'creative activities' should be timetabled, that individuals – *all* individuals – should be expected to be creative to order, as it were, is itself not a little strange. True, many gifted artists have produced works of quality when commissioned to write, say, an ode or an overture; but it has hardly been laid down that they should do so at, even if by, a certain time.

We need also, especially when considering a general, as distinct from a specialized educational programme or optional activities, to examine the assertion that in order to get on the 'inside' of artistic understanding pupils should be enabled (indeed, presumably, required) to '"get their coats off" and to "do" the arts themselves' (ibid. para. 18). This might seem to have a nice hearty ring about it and to suggest a thoroughly down-to-earth approach. But it is unfortunately apt to suggest that appreciation is a rather more nebulous affair and does not involve anything nearly so active and involving or so demanding of effort. Doubtless there may be enormous difficulties for any teacher who tries to bring about that alert yet absorbed kind of looking or listening or reading that I have characterized as aesthetic (not least in a society in which everyone is bombarded by images, piped music and printed matter at almost every turn). But because in such situations pupils do not necessarily have their coats off or their sleeves rolled up it does not follow that they may not be strenuously engaged – 'doing' in a most important sense.

Moreover, it is not *logically* necessary in order to understand and enjoy any of the arts to participate in either art-making or performance. On the contrary, to create something under the concept of art presupposes that it is something to be contemplated: the notion of spectator enjoyment is logically prior to that of participant enjoyment (Strawson, 1974). And this is surely borne out in actual experience: many people have never written a novel or directed a film or composed an opera, say, yet might want to claim that they nevertheless can appreciate novels, films, operas, etc., as art.

There is, indeed, an important respect in which art-making is not only not opposed to appreciation, but actually requires it. In contrast to the situation in which pupils are simply provided with art materials (using the term in a broad sense) and then left alone merely to explore possibilities without concern for what results, there is always within genuine creative activity in the arts a certain 'onlooker' element. (How otherwise would an artist, once embarked on a work, be able to proceed or to say that it was finished?) As Wollheim (1968, para. 47) points out – albeit in the context of a different discussion – while not all spectators are artists, all artists are spectators. In this respect, he suggests, it is a mistake to contrast the two, as if there were two classes of people; rather, there are two roles which can be fulfilled by the same individual.

We should, however, notice that Wollheim says '*can* be fulfilled' (in keeping with his previous remark), and that this is a point not be be confused with a different one: the absurd claim, originally stemming from the artist Eric Gill, and since foolishly seized on as a slogan by some writers on education, namely, that 'the artist is not a special kind of person; but every person is a special kind of artist'. Such a sentiment, D. J. O'Connor (1982) suggests, was no doubt inspired by Gill's Christian egalitarianism and was expressed some fifty years in advance of our present humanist egalitarianism; but it is no less fatuous for all that. And one does not have to subscribe to

O'Connor's general thesis of education as put forward here, or restrict the term 'artist' to geniuses such as Shakespeare or Mozart, to agree on this point. If everyone is to be considered an artist in as much as he composes a few lines of verse from time to time or hums tunes of his own making, everyone is also to be considered a scientist – a special sort, of course! – in as much as he asks questions about why certain things in the world are as they are, or a special sort of historian in virtue of his habit of recounting the events of his day at school or at home, and so on. On such a view, 'artist' becomes emptied of all significant meaning, and the special achievements of gifted and hard-working dramatists, choreographers, composers, and the like, underrated.

None of this is to deny that attempts at art-making might stimulate interest in and perhaps assist understanding of works such as the individual could not even dream of composing or that are beyond his ability to perform. To gain first-hand experience of wrestling with a particular medium as one endeavours to structure a piece might well sharpen perception of certain details and subtleties of meaning in a work of which one might otherwise not have been so readily aware; or, perhaps, of how it is in some way flawed. It might, indeed, seem rather strange if such experience did *not* prompt pupils to take an interest in and become more capable of responding appropriately to works of art; similarly, in the case of performing. Nevertheless, while there might seem to be some evidence as regards the motivational value of such procedures, as cited in *The Arts in Schools* (para. 58), for example, there is no reason for thinking, as implied here, that it *must* be the case. Neither is it necessarily the best way. The matter is an empirical one, though not at all easy to settle. For it would have to be shown – and by far more rigorous and large-scale investigations than any that have so far been undertaken – that interest could not as successfully have been awakened and developed by any other means. If, meanwhile, we continue to hope that all this *might* happen and that it affords some justification for all pupils engaging in creative activity, then such activity has to be linked, regularly and systematically, with the appreciation of particular works, and its value thus recognized chiefly in terms of its serving that end if it is aesthetic education that is being undertaken.

A criticism to be taken seriously, however, is that much of what goes on in schools at present in the name of 'creative activities' tends to result in many pupils remaining relatively ignorant of and indifferent towards the fine arts, let alone capable of discriminating appraisal. Part of the problem here is that it is apt to be assumed that if, for example, children are moving to music or other sound patterns, making up stories or drawing (which poses particular problems here – see Meeson, 1972), they are necessarily engaged in *art*. But, unless they are enabled to regard what they produce from an artistic point of view and to become progressively aware of and concerned with artistic standards, whatever is in hand will be either activity which involves not so much imaginative effort of the kind characteristic of aesthetic awareness, as indulgence in sensuous experience or fantasy, or else some other kind of pursuit altogether (as, for instance, recording observations of something).

This is not to say, of course, that what goes on during 'creative activity' periods might not be of educational value in a variety of ways other than artistic or aesthetic. There might, for example, be a reinforcing of learning in other fields; social and physical benefits and the acquiring of various sorts of technical skills; or there might be therapeutic effects – the building up of confidence in speaking aloud through dramatic improvization, say – that could *facilitate* education. But if such possible outcomes are set up as specific aims experience of a distinctively artistic kind may well be missed. Moreover, they might result also in connection with other curriculum subjects. On the other hand, some artistic activities engaged in *as* artistic activities may, in virtue of their particular character, have built-in additional values – as, for example, the physical exercise provided by dance.

In the case of young children, however, it would be a matter for some surprise if, to begin with, interest in an end-product of their 'creative' pursuits took precedence over enjoyment of the sheer act of, say, applying paint to paper or beating a drum, or of an activity involving co-operation or interaction with others. It is also perfectly right and proper that pupils should value any artistic skills they may have and take a pride in (among other achievements) their artistic accomplishments. But while creative activities may help to satisfy, if only temporarily, the need to feel they count for something, ultimately – as in any area – they have to be helped towards a realistic self-assessment. For there to be aesthetic education, the focus has increasingly to be not on the self or the group, not so much on *my* poem, *our* mural, doing things 'My Way', but on *this poem, this mural*, etc.

However, to be able to regard what one has made as something which, when finished, belongs to the public world, and which, if it is art, is *of its nature* up for appraisal by others, for *their* interest and enjoyment too, is an achievement of some sophistication. Similarly with performing. And, while aesthetic experience may help to promote moral development, aesthetic development is, in turn, to some extent dependent on the growth of moral sensibility. Not only children but also some adults may remain stuck at the stage of being overridingly concerned with *their* 'own thing', *their* performance. Dancers, singers and actors, by virtue of the fact that the works they present are manifest through their own person, are perhaps especially liable to a preoccupation with self that can border on narcissism: techniques of performance can all too easily be *flaunted*, rather than *used* in the service of a work.

Indeed, John Wilson (1978) insists that the limiting factor in the development of aesthetic awareness is a lack of the ability or desire to put oneself (that 'fat, relentless ego' in Iris Murdoch's phrase) in the background. Perhaps all the more difficult, it might be suggested, in the case of one's own creative achievements, which, understandably, usually have a highly personal significance; and it is impossible without frequent exposure to works that arouse wonder, admiration, and depth of thought and feeling.

In the attempt to direct attention outward to the created form, therefore, one task of the teacher will be to foster the capacity of most children to take delight not merely in random assortments of colours, textures, tones, movements, etc., but in striking configurations of such elements. The young child's love of mere repetition, for instance, typically displayed in the context of his encountering the same story or song, say, demanded over and over again, can gradually be extended to more subtle repetitions that lead to telling contrasts, variations and climaxes *within* stories, poems, etc. Many folk and popular songs are valuable here, often providing excellent examples of binary, ternary, and other simple compositional forms.

Children engaged in creative endeavours of their own may also be helped to use such forms and devices themselves as they become progressively more concerned with producing well structured pieces, however short. Clearly, considerable sensitivity and sympathetic judgement on the part of the teacher are needed here as regards when to encourage spontaneity, exploration, and a relatively uninhibited response to a stimulus, how much time to devote to the practice of techniques, when to allow work to remain in an unfinished or improvised state, and when to insist on more exact formulation. But, unless such formulation is eventually regularly called for, unless patience, persistence and the acquisition of the necessary skills are cultivated, and unless pupils learn to build on ideas, rather than merely produce one novelty after another or string ideas or technical exercises together in any order, the attitudes developed are likely to remain of a self-regarding nature and aesthetic development stunted.

In order, then, for pupils to make that kind of response – thoughtful and at the same time felt – that is characteristic of aesthetic awareness, they have, for example, to be presented with a range of possibilities from which careful selection has to be made, to have their attention drawn to various ways in which something has been achieved that are interesting and appropriate to whatever is being attempted, and required to stand back from time to time and reflect on what they or others are producing or have produced. In any case, it would be unfortunate if the 'first, fine careless rapture' of setting off on the adventure of art-making were thought to be the only exciting and pleasurable part of the enterprise, and all that follows mere drudgery. As Mary Wigman, the distinguished German dancer/choreographer, once remarked: 'There are not only the intoxicating moments of conceiving the image. There is also the ecstasy of sober work' (1966, p. 13). And children are more capable of that particular sort of 'ecstasy' than perhaps many teachers suppose.

## Expression, Expressiveness and Communication

Deflecting attention from the self to the work, or the work-in-the-making, may also be assisted in creative activity by pupils experimenting with well tried techniques of invention in the various art forms as a contrast to having always to begin from some personal experience outside art. And here, in view of the deeply ingrained assumption on the part of most teachers (and others) that an art work invariably springs from its author's actual emotions and thoughts – an idea that would have been unintelligible before the eighteenth century and that even today is foreign to Chinese and Indian art theory – the possibility needs to be stressed that inspiration may be derived from the medium itself. Many a poet and writer of 'lyrics', for instance, has often found an appropriate thought as a result of finding a rhyme or playing with words in other ways – by reversal, assonance, etc.; as, indeed, many children enjoy doing, especially at certain stages. Similarly, just two or three shapes or intervals or contrasting group formations of dancers, say, can become the basis of a composition which, far from being devoid of feeling, is charged with expressive quality.

Often, of course, a work does have its origin in a deeply moving experience or some other aspect of an artist's life; but it is only one of many possible starting points. It is also only one way in which a work might correctly be said to be expressive, and to characterize artistic activity exclusively in terms of the creative artist's thoughts and feelings at a particular time (even if it is not erroneously supposed that these are freely poured out, as in shouts of rage or tears of sorrow) reveals an inadequate understanding of both the concept of expression and that of art. For the expressiveness of a great deal of music, as well as of architecture and abstract paintings and sculptures, can be understood without reference to such thoughts and feelings. Rather, it has to do with the imaginatively perceived qualities of the work (Tormey, 1971). To hear a nocturne as full of longing, for example, is not to say that the composer was necessarily full of longing either during or before its composition. Neither does the aesthetically aware listener or performer necessarily experience an actual feeling of longing (though it would be odd if no one ever did: the frequent usage in much arts criticism of the language of mental states is not merely arbitrary or accidental).

There is thus a distinction to be drawn between that use of 'expression' where it makes sense to ask 'What is expressed?'

(and where an answer might be, say, grief or defiance) and that where the question is quite out of place (Scruton, 1983, ch. 6). In the first case, an art work might be an expression of (that is, the artist intentionally expresses some particular idea or emotion); in the second, rather as someone might not actually feel, for instance, irritable or amused, yet have or 'wear' an irritable or amused *look* – an air or, as we say, an expression, of irritation or amusement – so some art works may have a jubilant or restless quality, but not be an expression of the artist's jubilation or restlessness on a particular occasion. It is possible therefore to savour the expressiveness of a piece without either knowing or believing that it was directly related to a specific experience of the artist. Nor need a musician or a dancer have such information in order to perform a work 'with expression'; and if he went through the gamut of feelings expressed every time he performed the work he would probably be too exhausted to continue. Rather, in bringing out its expressive *qualities*, he sings or plays or dances *with understanding*: his knowledge is thus, as Scruton further insists, a species of practical, not theoretical knowledge.

Hence, if a teacher (somewhat vaguely) tells pupils to put some expression into their singing or playing or dancing, he does not expect them to go away and have some actual experience akin to that to be perceived in the music or the dance, then come back and somehow try to discharge it into the piece. Instead (if he knows his job), he will on the one hand find ways of appealing to their imagination, and on the other draw attention to details such as the appropriate phrasing, placing of accents and pauses, the tempo, increase and decrease of vigour, and suchlike – often indicated in a score by what, significantly, are called 'expression marks' (but which nevertheless allow a measure of freedom of interpretation).

In the case of some representational works both the expression of certain ideas or feelings *and* expressive quality may be involved. A painting which depicts a scene of jollity, for example, may be gay and energetic too in its formal features – its rhythms, lines, colours, etc.; or, by contrast, may deal with its subject matter in such a way as to merit ascriptions such as 'sly', 'compassionate' or 'cool and detached' (cf. Sircello, 1972). That is, the artist's treatment of his theme may give a work an expressiveness over and above that which belongs to the depicted scene, situation or characters. (A pupil's creative efforts or a performance, then, that are somewhat confused or sentimental, for instance, cannot be reasonably defended by his referring to the confusion or sentimentality of the subject-matter!)

A good deal of the literature of aesthetic education, however, remains saturated with one or other variety – often something of a mishmash – of those expression theories of art which with the upsurge of Romanticism succeeded mimetic theories of the eighteenth century, and which placed overriding importance on the state of mind of the creative artist. (Such theories are not, of course, to be confused with Expressionist *movements* in the various arts – as, for example, those associated with Kandinsky and Munch in painting and Schoenberg in music.) Along with some kinds of expression theory, educational discourse also often retains something of early organic theory (later versions of which became more object-centred); and this was reinforced by twentieth-century psycho-analytic doctrines about art-making having its roots in the unconscious and burgeoning forth from a freely creative individual by a mysterious process thought to resemble the spontaneous growth of a living organism. This is much in evidence in Read's writings, for instance, and often associated too with talk of 'self-expression', 'self-realization', 'growth', etc., in educational literature.

The idea of artistic activity as the expression of personal feeling is also typically coupled with the idea of art as a vehicle for communication. Thus *The Arts in Schools*, for example, while rightly pointing out the error of dividing feeling from intellect and reason, and of regarding the arts as outpourings of emotion (para. 7c), nevertheless claims that they are '*natural* forms of expression and communication' (para. 66, italics given). Now assertions about what is natural to human beings are notoriously problematic, all too often in this context signalling a readiness to overlook or underrate the *social* character of a great deal of human development and achievement; and here, clearly, is a failure to take account of the social and historical nature of art (as discussed in Chapter 3) and the vitally important role played in art-making by an understanding of certain artistic styles and traditions. Several references here to art from the past, like talk of 'the weight of the centuries' and of tradition being 'less useful now' (*Curriculum 11–16*, pp. 36–7), also betray a tendency to confuse tradition with convention, and to suppose that works of our own time can adequately be appreciated in isolation from what has gone before and a personal style developed independently of established practice (cf. Scruton, 1979, ch. 7; 1983, chs 2 and 10; Baxter, 1983).

Further, it is only in a metaphorical sense that the various arts might be said to be *languages* – an assumption that often accompanies talk about art as expression and communication. This is not the place to consider in detail the enormously complex and controversial nature of language, but a point of crucial importance to the present discussion is that one of the major functions that a genuine language must be able to fulfil is that of imparting facts, of stating what is the case. Linguistic meaning has an essential connection with matters of truth and falsity – precisely that which, on a view of the aesthetic as involving imaginative, not ordinary perception, is not the case with artistic meaning. Even with literature there is a distinction to be drawn between *literal* and *literary* meaning. As Wittgenstein succinctly puts it, 'a poem, even though it is composed in the language of information, is not used in the language-game of giving information' (1967, para. 160). In so far as we might remark in the presence of a work, 'How true!', it is typically when we seem to find confirmation or illumination of something *we already know*, or only partly understand: we have it brought home to us, 'proved on the pulses', in Keats's vivid phrase (I shall return to this point in a moment).

Consequently, what is sometimes referred to as 'acquiring a vocabulary' in a particular art form – again, necessarily a metaphor – is not like learning a system of signs for which there are verbal equivalents, with standard meanings determined by rules and conventions of usage. If, indeed, the arts *were* languages, the notions of freedom and originality as they apply in art would be out of place, for the artist would be constrained in a way that determined how, once he had started, he could or could not continue (as in the construction of a sentence).

Another claim often met with in connection with talk about the arts as languages, or as forms of expression and communication – especially, perhaps, in the case of music and dance – is that they are more effective and more powerful than words. Yet it is in words that such claims are – necessarily – expressed and communicated. Those who make them, sometimes in the course of seeking to challenge the strong linguistic tradition in British education (as, once again, the chairman of the Gulbenkian *Report on Dance Education* (p. VIII), for example), therefore argue against their own case, employing the very means they tend to disparage (cf. Best, 1978, ch. 9). Some passionate advocates of the arts in education even go so far as to claim that they are universal languages, more easily understood by 'ordinary' people than genuine language is. But this again is to fail to recognize the socio-historical character of art and the difficulties of appreciating in any depth the art of a culture whose traditions and ways of life are vastly different from one's own.

Expression and communication theories of art also often lead some people to suppose that, since we all spontaneously reveal actual feelings through the body, the dance in particular is an art form in which everyone can easily be creative. 'Every child can dance', it is confidently proclaimed in the DES publication *Movement: Physical Education in the Primary Years* (p. 44); patently, not an empirical claim (how would it ever be tested?), but a naïve expression of beliefs about, first, 'the child' and, second, the dance – as revealed in what follows: 'The sharpness of his senses and the intensity of his reactions frequently demand immediate expression. He bursts into movement which being charged with feeling has the essential quality of dance. When spontaneous expression of this sort becomes clearly defined it can truly be called dance' (note the 'truly' heralding what amounts to a persuasive definition).

What frequently escapes notice is that the scope (and limitations) of the various art media are largely determined by the social milieu in which they are used. Strange as it might perhaps seem initially, certain feelings might not even be available to members of a particular community, though when a highly innovative artist breaks with certain conventions to explore and conquer new territory he may help to develop and change the consciousness of that group. Even his work, however, grows out of the thinking and feeling typical of the period and society to which he belongs. If therefore it be asked, Huw Morris-Jones suggests, *whose* feelings a work of art expresses, it may be answered that it is those who 'speak and feel in a common language, who have learnt the rules, techniques and conventions which are features of the specialized artistic "languages" of this society' (1968, p. 103). Thus, anyone deprived of such learning is deprived of whole areas of affective experience – a consideration frequently ignored by those who advocate 'free expression' without interference in arts education. As David Best puts it, 'a person with only trite forms of expression is a person who is capable of only trite possibilities of experience' (1979, p. 218).

There are other serious problems about conceiving of the arts as 'the most natural means' of meeting the *need* of young people to organize feelings and ideas about experience (*The Arts in Schools*, para. 7f) and as 'an externalizing of what the pupil feels, knows and is able to do' (*Curriculum 11–16*, p. 36). For it is apt to suggest that there are already in existence fully fledged thoughts and feelings, private and unobservable, which then get *ex-pressed, projected into* words, gestures, paint, etc., so that these then *embody* them. But what is not considered here is how, before the making of the play, the collage, or whatever it might be, a specific idea or mood or emotion can be identified. The assumption seems to be that the 'inner' is somehow clearly distinguishable *apart* from the 'outer' – a misconception from which theories of expression and communication typically suffer. Hence the potential danger of talk about art as an 'objective presentation of subjectivity' (Langer, 1953, 1957), or as 'externalizing inner experience' (Phenix, 1964), or as 'meaning-embodied' (Arnaud Reid, 1969).

Arnaud Reid, it is true, is at pains to insist that it would be quite inaccurate to suggest that 'what is discovered in or after the expressive act is *what was there all the time*' (p. 44). Rather, as he says, what is brought into being is something completely new, with new feelings, new meanings, 'specifically embodied in this thing here before us, nowhere else and never before' (p. 62). Nevertheless, to ask 'how the experience, meaning and knowledge of life outside the arts influences, "enters", "gets into" and is at the same time transformed by the aesthetic into a new dimension' (p. 41) does seem to presuppose the prior existence of something else. If, however, we take the work of art as a criterion of a certain feeling, Best (1974, p. 189) argues, 'the problem, in that formulation, dissolves – it cannot be posed, for we do not have two entities, therefore there is no difficulty about getting them together'.

Yet this is not, it seems to me, to say that before or during the composition of a piece an artist may not be aware, however vaguely, of ill-defined ideas or feelings, as yet inchoate and out of reach, that seem to cry out for articulation – 'partial formulations, schematic forms, floating images', as Reid has it (1969, p. 75). What may sometimes happen in art-making is thus not unlike the experience we commonly have when we grope for and eventually find – or perhaps are offered – a word or phrase that enables us to say exactly what we mean, and so to discover just what we do think or feel. Without that precise formulation it was indeed impossible for us to know what this was. In this respect, then, what is required in a good deal of creative endeavour in the arts is not, as frequently claimed, *divergent* but *convergent* thinking: the search for *this* particular word, shade of colour, cadence, and the like is a narrowing down (cf. Symes, 1983).

Such experiences can therefore be peculiarly satisfying for the individual concerned and may be felt as an escape from or an overcoming of the burdens of the unknown and the formless – 'the general mess of imprecision of feeling,/Undisciplined squads of emotion', in Eliot's words, following his powerful image of each such venture as 'a raid on the inarticulate' (*East Coker*, V); or perhaps there is a sense of ease and freedom, as with Wordsworth's 'a timely utterance gave that thought relief' ('Intimations of Immortality' Ode). And the presently fashionable talk of 'getting things together' is perhaps some indication of a deep-seated satisfaction that many human beings find in things that are well ordered and integrated.

To enlarge a learner's 'vocabulary' in a particular art form, then, and to provide him with the skills and knowledge necessary for composing within that discipline is to make available to him a means whereby his experience might become increasingly differentiated and understood. But this is not to say that everyone is equally capable of taking advantage of such means; and if, lacking sufficient talent, our attempt is such that, as

John Casey suggests, 'we do it in a way that is ridiculous, so that our choice of expression seems totally inappropriate to the feeling we wish to convey' (1973, p. 77), it can be singularly frustrating. Which is no doubt why some people cannot bear to be *amateur* painters, poets, dancers, and so on.

## Developing and Checking Aesthetic Understanding

The educating of feeling in the arts can, however, be achieved also – and to a greater extent – by enabling pupils to appreciate the works of mature artists to which they might reasonably be expected to respond at various stages, and which, indeed, often express just what an individual would like to have been able to express himself. Having tried their hand at a love poem, for instance, adolescents often find someone else's 'says it all' – and more – for them too. In clarifying and intensifying some shadowy, seemingly elusive experience, a work may also help us to realize that we do not suffer or rejoice (or whatever it may be) in isolation, yet at the same time have a highly personal significance. In J. M. Cameron's words, 'although we know that this poem that speaks to us and for us speaks also to and for others, it is still as though it speaks to us alone' (1962, p. 145). Perhaps even more strikingly, an art work may enable us to experience a certain elation, yearning or serenity – the words can only be approximate – which we have never encountered before.

The more opportunities we have then to become acquainted with works of merit, the greater the chance that our sensibilities will be expanded and enriched. Whether the experience is that of complete revelation, or more akin to the 'I have known it for a long time, but only now do I realize what it is' kind, which Elliott (1974) calls 'contemplative knowledge' (but extends beyond the arts), we might be said to *learn*, to come to *know* something. Yet it is not a matter of learning or coming to know *that* such and such is the case (as often seems to be implied in, for example, *The Arts in Schools* and the APU document). Rather than having a further item of information to add to our store of propositional knowledge, in art we are *shown*, helped to an *imaginative understanding* of something that is not precisely statable in any other way: what it might have been like, for instance, as revealed in some of Henry Moore's sketches, to sleep in the Underground during the Second World War; or, as in Cecil Day Lewis's *Walking Away*, for a parent to be separated from his son when the child first goes away to school.

This poem is a good example of how a closing line or lines (here, 'How selfhood begins with a walking away /And love is proved in the letting go') illumine the rest of the work, while at the same time requiring for their fuller understanding some grasp of what has gone before, as distinct, that is, from understanding merely their literal sense. On the other hand, it seems to me that many philosophers overstate their case when they draw attention to the importance of taking into account the context in which various details occur. Michael Weston, for instance, discussing *The Duchess of Malfi*, claims that 'one does not know whether a given line is beautiful or tragic independently of the context in which it occurs, and that context is provided by the structure of the play' (1975, p. 90). Yet the words that he quotes, 'Cover her face: mine eyes dazzle: she died young' – like 'After life's fitful fever he sleeps well', or 'Brightness falls from the air/Queens have died young and fair' – are, I would argue, beautiful, moving, and do have a tragic ring irrespective of whether they apply to the Duchess, to Duncan, Helen, or anyone else, no matter what the context. This is not to say that they do not have an added beauty and pathos – and greater *artistic* significance – when they are understood in relation to the rest of the work. But there are hundreds of lines of poetry, even handfuls of words (a list of Proust's place names or church spires, say), which may, like a detail from a fresco, a single gesture or an attitude or arabesque, strike us as majestic, graceful, or in some other way aesthetically powerful, even when isolated from their context. Indeed, it is by no means an uncommon experience to find snatches of poetry or music memorable and moving even if the rest of the work cannot be brought to mind; and there would seem to be an important place in schools for anthologies of quotations among which children might just 'wander' from time to time.

This kind of understanding that we gain in aesthetic encounters is often usefully compared with knowing a person. For, as well as knowing that someone is John Smith, together with certain other *facts* about him, I might also know him in such a way that in certain circumstances I say, 'That's not the John Smith I know' – that is, the person whom I normally perceive in a particular light, the (intentional) object of certain attitudes and feelings on my part (cf. Scruton, 1974, ch. 15); and it is sometimes known as 'acquaintance-knowledge' or 'experiential-knowledge' (for example, Reid, 1961, 1969, 1973). Further, just as it would be a misunderstanding of what friendship is if we thought it involved making use of someone, so it is a misunderstanding of art if we suppose we go to it in order, as Collinson puts it, to 'learn lessons from the work, make practical applications out of it or calculatingly relate our experience of it to the everyday world' (1973, p. 202). Rather, in cases where we do learn, we do so *gratuitously*.

How then can another person – a teacher, for instance – know whether or not an individual has gained such understanding in the case of art? How is he to know what someone evidently engrossed in a book, a film, a piece of music, etc., is 'making' of it, *how* he is responding? To some extent 'evidence' may vary as between one art form and another. In the performing arts and in literature, for example, a pupil might be able to indicate something of his response in his performance of the work. Wittgenstein asks, 'Isn't understanding shown in the expression with which someone reads the poem, sings the tune?', and answers confidently: 'Certainly' (1967, para. 171). But lack of adequate skill is an obvious drawback here; nor can an individual be expected to demonstrate in this way his understanding of *every* role in a play or a dance, *every* vocal or instrumental line of a composition, etc. On the other hand, a technically accurate performance is not incompatible with a certain lack of feeling – though the absence or presence of warmth and sincerity do seem detectable by experienced observers and listeners (a panel of 'assessors', rather than a single individual, however, would seem to be the ideal).

Again, the choices that pupils make if they compile their own anthologies, collect reproductions and photographs, bring along favourite records, and so forth, are – provided that they are genuine choices – likely to be revealing. As Casey points out, 'finding – or for that matter, writing – a maudlin poem to express one's grief cannot be considered just an accident, a quirk of behaviour . . . the choice is governed by a conception of the object' (1973, p. 75). To take account of a range of cases over a period, then, can help to build up a picture of an individual's appreciative capabilities and of his aesthetic development. Perhaps from time to time – as, indeed, even among people we might justifiably call 'aesthetically educated' – there may be lapses of taste (using that term in the sense of having to do with discrimination and judgement, not merely personal preference). Yet a lapse does presuppose some level of consistency. In any case, as far as aesthetic education in the arts is concerned, there is often a useful place for the relatively inconsequential in order for young people to get going at all. The educator has to move, as Arnaud Reid says, *'from* where the pupil is, *towards* something more discriminating, finer, richer, fuller, more complex' (1973, p. 81).

It might, for example, be helpful in the early stages, as Wilson (1978) suggests, to encourage comparisons between good and bad instances of well-known and well-liked inventions that have a recognizable *form* – jokes, riddles, graffiti, and the like – so that children are brought to see that the 'same' thing can be done well or badly. What, for instance, makes this limerick sloppy or neat, this Western tedious or dramatic, this line of a song predictable or sentimental while that one has an unexpected twist or in some other way departs from the stereotype?

Nevertheless, Saw is right to question whether 'the plain man' really does always know what he likes (1972, p. 23). Certainly he can only like or dislike what he knows; and it is clearly the job of education to extend children's horizons so that they have at least a glimpse of what lies beyond the presently fashionable, the hackneyed, the trivial and the obvious – beyond that which lacks subtlety and complexity, where there are always happy endings, clear-cut 'goodies' that always triumph over clear-cut 'baddies', or conversely, where only sordid caricatures of men and women are presented (cf. Hepburn, 1972). For there is nothing, as Michael Oakeshott points out, to encourage us to believe that 'what has captured current fancy is the most valuable part of our inheritance' (1967, p. 161); and the releasing of pupils from servitude to the current dominant feelings, emotions, images, ideas, etc., of which both he and Hepburn speak seems especially necessary in the case of much (though not all) popular art.

Sometimes, anyway, it may be a good deal more effective for a teacher who is himself fired with enthusiasm for a particular work of a kind unfamiliar to his pupils to plunge them in at the deep end and try to carry them along with him before subjecting the piece *and* his responses to critical scrutiny, rather than first attempt to get them to examine with similar rigour items of the sort with which they are familiar, and on whose behalf they may tend to take up defensive attitudes. Comparisons and contrasts between works (and jokes, etc.) of quality can, however, play a vital role: put Ted Hughes's *Fish* beside Yeats's *Byzantium*, for example, and the brisk, urgent and erratic movement of the one may point up even more vividly the grand, spacious sweep of the other.

Whatever a teacher's strategies, it is essential that children are encouraged from an early age to talk about pieces both that they themselves make or choose and that are presented to them. Collinson (who provides a somewhat exaggeratedly purist account of the aesthetic such that she herself is aware might give an impression of 'an altogether too glaring and blinkered attitude' (1973, p. 207)), characterizes the aesthetically educated person in terms of an individual who stands in rapt contemplation in front of, say, a painting but who may or may not be able to 'talk about, describe or *comment* on certain objects and situations in a certain way' (p. 197). She is, of course, right that comments dealing exclusively with technical details are not a sufficient criterion of aesthetic involvement; but for the purposes of *educating*, discussion (which might include reference to technical aspects) is vital both to the fostering of such experience and to attempts to check, as far as this is possible, whether it has been achieved.

There may, of course, be occasions when a piece is left to make its own impact, with little said either by way of introduction or follow-up (as also with children's own pieces): a teacher's silences, like his stillnesses, can be as eloquent as – and sometimes more eloquent than – his words and gestures. It is also important to remember that one needs time to *live* in 'the aesthetic moment' and to develop acquaintance with a work, rather than always move on to something else or make a verbal response to it or attend to someone else's. Pursuing the analogy with getting to know a person, Collinson insists that this is spoiled if a third party stands alongside delivering information about that person (p. 210). Yet it is often helpful if he is *introduced*, and while on some occasions there might be an immediate *rapprochement*, on others one may feel strange and at a loss to know how to proceed. Here the analogy breaks down, for in contrast to a person a work can only 'stand' there, so to speak, awaiting a further effort on the part of the other. Moreover, delivering information is not all of, and not even chiefly, what is required in arousing and furthering aesthetic involvement, though it may have an important place by way of preparation for and later study of a piece. The situation is typically unlike that mentioned by Harry Broudy in respect of Eliot, for whom the ideal critic was one who put before him something that he had never before encountered and then left him alone with it, relying on his own sensibility, intelligence and capacity for wisdom. 'That's fine for T. S. Eliot, who already had well-developed sensibility, intelligence, and capacity for wisdom', remarks Broudy, 'precisely that which the pupil does not yet have' (1972, p. 105).

Now at first what children say about a story, a song, a piece of sculpture, etc., may be little more than 'Fantastic!', 'It's very pretty', 'I liked that part where . . .' (or, alternatively, 'It's boring', 'It left me cold'), and so on. But at least it is appropriate that a personal response is elicited and expressed – so long as, that is, this is neither a piece of self-deception (as, for example, when what one enjoys or dislikes is, rather, some association aroused by the piece), nor insincere in being calculated merely to please or impress or conform to expectations, or, by contrast, to shock or annoy teachers and (or) peers: a problem, however, that is not peculiar to the aesthetic situation, but has much wider implications (social, psychological, etc).

Nevertheless, in order that progress be achieved towards more differentiated responses, more acutely discriminating perceptions, together with consideration of whether those responses are, or are not, justifiable *in terms of the object*, it is essential that a suitable vocabulary is built up. For without some means of reference both to ordinarily observable details and to aesthetic qualities not only is understanding restricted as regards how others respond, and why, but also one's own powers of perception are limited: that for which we have no adequate terminology is likely to be missed. Hence the need for pupils to become familiar with certain technical terms, and perhaps in music and dance, notational symbols (in both cases there are simplified forms for learning crucial concepts), as well as with that imaginative use of words that is characteristic of aesthetic discussion. (All this applies too, of course, in connection with art-making and performance.)

There would seem to be an especially important need for a technical vocabulary in respect of architecture and sculpture, for ordinary language is somewhat impoverished in names for shapes and spatial configurations – a factor that may contribute to the difficulty many people appear to find in appreciating the three-dimensional arts other than as regards any representational interest they may have (see, on sculpture, Rogers, 1968, 1969). Similarly in the case of dance, which is still apt to be approached largely as a musical or a dramatic art (cf. Redfern, 1976, 1984).

The use of language in aesthetic appraisals as such is, of course, often far less exact. Yet it would be wrong to suppose that language that is suggestive rather than precise, or rich in emotive power and association, is inappropriate for the purpose (cf. Reid, 1969, ch. 1). On the contrary, the use of imagery, simile and metaphor (for example, chunky harmonies, swirling arpeggios, flinty rhythms), of expressions which have their natural home in talk about human attributes and mental states (for example, a despairing or triumphant chord, the nervous or resolute lines of a drawing, a gauche or poised literary piece), of words and phrases that might seem to stop short at a concern with craftsmanship and skill (for example, a roughly hewn sonata movement, a finely wrought plot) is the *sort* of linguistic device which serves to guide ear and eye, to reveal and open up fresh perceptions, to communicate both subtle nuances or defects and the overall flavour of a piece. And it is some indication of aesthetic development when pupils become able to employ language in this manner, making more sparing and more judicious use of, for instance, 'lovely', 'horrible', 'nice', 'ghastly', and applying a greater variety of terms to music and dance in particular than those old war-horses 'jolly' and 'sad'. The possibility of their picking up clichés and of parroting what others say, or merely making what they take to be the 'right noises' has, clearly, to be borne in mind. On the other hand, children's sincerity and the nature of their responses are often manifest in what to the adult may seem unexpected ascriptions or in those of their own invention (for example, 'a wiggly, scarifying tune').

To move back and forth between the more straightforwardly descriptive and the more evaluative uses of language is, as we have already seen, a characteristic feature of discussion which involves the attempted justification of aesthetic appraisals. And here the educator faces a most challenging task. For by their very nature aesthetic appraisals are always subject to revision, and, in the case of the arts, further knowledge about works from the past, together with changing social and cultural values, may make for the significance of now this aspect of a work, now that, being highlighted in such a way that it might seem as if in this realm everyone's view is as good as the next one's. The teacher, then, has to try to create the sort of atmosphere and conditions which favour what Collinson calls a 'respectful, welcoming attitude' towards an art work (or a child's piece). Yet, while it is desirable to extend 'patience and favour' (in Elliott's phrase) to each one, there are limits. 'To suspend judgement may be a virtue,' remarks Eva Schaper (commenting on Elliott), 'to suspend it indefinitely may often be not to say what one thinks' (1972, p. 139). Thus pupils have to be helped, on the one hand, to 'give' themselves to a work without, however, allowing it simply to 'wash over' them; on the other, to maintain a certain distance from it yet without making a clinical or slick assessment.

The aim within a general education is not, of course, to produce professional critics any more than it is to produce professional artists or performers. Nevertheless, there has to be a commitment (I would claim) to the developing of individuals who are prepared to entertain new ideas and feelings and at the same time are capable of independent judgement. It may, however, be far from easy to get them beyond the stage of merely disagreeing with others. Stock responses among older pupils such as 'That's middle-class', 'decadent', 'out of date', 'not relevant', etc., may all too readily be forthcoming without any further attempt on the speaker's part either to say exactly what he means or to support his opinions by means of comparisons or contrasts, references to observable features of the work, and so forth. ('That's a value judgement!' seems often to be trotted out, once the term is acquired, as a label for that about which nothing more can be said – as if it *precluded* rather than *made way* for rational discussion, and with little inkling, it need hardly be said, of the problematic nature of the fact/value distinction.)

Without critical reflection, however, there can be no such thing as aesthetic education: it is part of that larger task which the educator in a liberal/democratic tradition cannot shirk – the task of fostering the give-and-take of informed discussion, which involves not only confidence and skill in expressing and defending one's own views but also a readiness to listen to those of others and to be prepared to reconsider and perhaps change one's initial stance. It is precisely his concern for (and what should be his expertise in dealing with) this aspect of arts education that will make any educator pause before handing over his job to professional artists, no matter how skilled they be in their sphere (as proposed, for instance, in the Gulbenkian *Report on Dance Education*). Moreover, critical appreciation may be linked in practical ways with pupils' own artistic activities – providing verbal introductions, planning catalogues, writing programme notes, résumés, reviews, and the like.

Given the nature of the critical enterprise, however, and also the assumptions and traditions that have prevailed for so long in many schools, as well as in teacher-education, it might seem easier and more enjoyable for some, teachers and learners alike, if 'creative' work takes precedence over 'appreciation'. But it does not follow that *as arts education* it is ultimately as important. There is probably a case for young children having the opportunity to participate in 'making and doing' with a variety of arts materials, though such a case may well rest on considerations other than those to do with art; and the time often spent in sheer organization before and after lessons might well give pause for reflection as to their precise aims and values. Attempts at art-making might also prove refreshing and profitable with pupils who suffer from programmes in, say, music and literature that are geared to examination requirements in such a way that many merely reproduce received opinion or ways of approaching particular works (though bad teaching of this kind may well extend to endeavours to promote creative activity). Yet while pupils' own efforts may be interesting, original and exciting, they may also be repetitive, cliché-ridden and dull; and they can hardly be expected to be – nor, typically, are they – profound or disturbing, capable of transporting others, of jolting them out of established patterns of thought and feeling, of illuminating and extending an understanding of the human condition. To deny young people first-hand acquaintance with great art, exposing them only to the products and performances of their peers, is clearly to leave them imprisoned within the straitjacket of their own necessarily limited experience.

Moreover, the capacity to respond to mature works and performances usually far outruns the capacity to create and perform mature works: most individuals whose own efforts are obviously not of the calibre of acknowledged masterpieces are nevertheless often able, particularly with the help of someone more knowledgeable and experienced, to appreciate at least some aspects of those masterpieces. Martha Graham, for example, tells of how a boy of eight once wrote to her saying how much he liked her dance *Lamentation*, but added that he thought it too short. On thinking it over however, he said, he supposed you could not feel such sorrow for any length of time. Here, then, we have a child capable not only of responding to a work that might not have been thought especially suitable for that age but of reflecting on it, as well as on his experience of it, albeit at the level simply of liking.

The loss on the part of many older pupils, so often deplored by teachers, of their earlier freshness, enthusiasm and general readiness to 'have a go' at making and doing in the arts might, indeed, be better regarded as a potential gain – a gain in terms of greater powers of self-criticism, more realistic self-assessment and increasing awareness of standards. What seems to be dissatisfaction with an activity is frequently, in fact, dissatisfaction with themselves, their own amateurish and perhaps rather pedestrian achievements, as their horizons expand and change. It may also result, as Reid points out, from some teachers, obsessed with ideas about expression, freedom, and the fear of 'imposing' anything on pupils, falling into the trap of imposing of another kind – the imposition on adolescents of methods suitable only for young children (1969, p. 271).

Similarly as regards performing in music and dance. And here the length of time required for the acquisition of skill and for sustained practice within even one branch or style of dance and with most instruments is such that within a general educational programme relatively little progress is likely to be achieved without other arts being neglected. Yet, lacking an introduction to a *range* of arts and genres, pupils can build up only a limited, perhaps even distorted, concept of art or even of one particular art form. And to be restricted to those which have traditionally featured most prominently in 'creative activities' has meant that many children have grown up with little, if any, critical appreciation of, for example, architecture and those twentieth-century arts of cinema, radio and television which so powerfully surround them everywhere. Further, since each art form, indeed each work, has a unique contribution to make to the education of feeling, there would seem to be grounds in the case of a compulsory curriculum for a certain width of experience, as contrasted with optional courses in which pupils could pursue those activities in which they have a particular interest or ability to a greater depth.

It would certainly be mistaken to suppose that aesthetic discrimination in one art form automatically carries over to another, or that certain concepts apply, as it were, across the board. The idea that a developed sense of rhythm, phrasing, or other features of music, for example, inevitably makes for awareness of comparable features of dance or poetry is just not borne out in practice: there are many lovers of music who seem to have little 'feeling' for either poetry or dance, while there are dancers who lack not only an ear for poetry (let alone a ready appreciation of its other aspects) but also musical discrimination – as witness how some choreographers use pieces of music. And any suggestion that appreciation of, say, the balance and unity of *The Winter's Tale* guarantees immediate appreciation of the balance and unity of Beethoven's Third Piano Concerto or

Constable's *The Hay Wain* is quite implausible. To insist once again, aesthetic concepts (that is, concepts functioning aesthetically) are not grasped intellectually and then applied over a variety of instances: appreciation of works even within the same art form requires judgement (in that sense which involves perception and thought in felt experience) *in each particular case*.

Nevertheless, this is often assisted by knowledge of a range of works of art and other objects of aesthetic interest. Moreover, rather as one may come to appreciate the singularity of a person as a result of acquaintance with several, and at the same time develop a richer concept of 'person' through knowing individuals, so in becoming familar with individual art works and increasingly aware of similarities and differences between them one both deepens understanding of the particular work and goes on building up one's concept of art.

# 6

# *Aesthetic Education outside the Arts*

It was suggested in the previous chapter that it would be unlikely that an individual would be considered aesthetically educated if he had no appreciation of at least some works of art. It may now be asked whether, conversely, if he were well acquainted with the arts but aesthetically indifferent to things outside art, his aesthetic education had been inadequate.

The authors of the APU document clearly believe that it would: 'We regard it as an important aspect of education that children should develop the capacity to make informed judgements about and respond appropriately to the aesthetic quality of natural and man-made environments' (para 2.4). They further claim that 'arts teaching in schools inevitably incurs a considerable responsibility in this sphere, as do other areas of the curriculum such as Craft, Design and Technology and Home Economics'.

Courses in these last-mentioned subjects would certainly seem to involve aesthetic appreciation of the particular sorts of objects with which they deal, and might even be seen as rather less than successful if they did not result in pupils becoming more perceptive also about the wider aspects of the environment in which those objects are set. Yet it seems somewhat optimistic to suppose (as implied in *Curriculum 11–16*, for example) that experience in craft, design and technology will necessarily extend to an aesthetic concern with the man-made environment in general; nor can development of aesthetic discrimination in home economics be expected to carry over to aesthetic appreciation of, say, feats of engineering skill.

And what of aesthetic awareness of natural phenomena? As the APU document suggests, the visual arts and poetry (in particular, perhaps) *can* help here; but again, not necessarily. Moreover, the reverse is equally possible. Indeed, one of the main inspirations for much landscape painting and the writing of 'nature poetry', one would have thought, is that landscapes, etc., are themselves already enjoyed aesthetically (though the influence of particular artistic traditions in the choice of subject should not be discounted). The claim, then, that 'the most effective and obvious way of encouraging a developing interest in aesthetic aspects of life is through the arts' (APU document, loc. cit.) is open to question. And it can hardly be overlooked that some artists and art connoisseurs are notoriously careless about dress and other aspects of personal appearance, and may not only pay little attention to things of aesthetic interest outside their particular artistic concerns but even take a positive stance against them. The former President of the Royal Academy, for instance, interviewed shortly before his retirement, declared that he would rather have concrete outside his window than tend a window box.

A distinction might be drawn, however, between the ability to take an aesthetic interest in certain kinds of things and the disposition to do so; and a general education has not necessarily failed if someone has been introduced to areas and avenues of experience which he later chooses not to pursue (there may be all sorts of good reasons for this). Nevertheless, in order that he becomes *able* to exercise choice in the aesthetic realm it may be asked whether there is not a range of such experience outside the arts, crafts and technology that is of educational importance. For while it seems widely accepted that (as we saw in Chapter 2) there are aspects of art that cannot be understood in terms of aesthetic appreciation of nature (for example), the possibility that there may be aspects of aesthetic awareness available in nature but not elsewhere does not seem to have been investigated very thoroughly either by philosophers or educationists.

A notable exception, however, is R. W. Hepburn, who in one of the few papers on this subject (originally published in 1963 and extended in 1966, now published in a collection (1984) which includes another of relevance here) argues persuasively that natural phenomena do indeed offer types of aesthetic experience that cannot be provided to the same extent, or even at all, by art. A range of feeling is opened up, he suggests, that the human scene by itself cannot evoke (Saw, indeed, claims to be moved more strongly by natural beauty than by the beauty of art – 1972, p. 25). Moreover, if aesthetic education fails to reckon with the differences that exist between the two areas and instils into the individual the expectations appropriate only to the appreciation of art, Hepburn maintains, that person 'will either pay very little aesthetic heed to natural objects, or else will heed them in the wrong way. He will look – and of course look in vain – for what can be found and enjoyed only in art' (1984, p. 16). (Such considerations have important consequences also for theorizing about the aesthetic mode of awareness: part of Hepburn's thesis is that the neglect of the study of natural beauty is a thoroughly bad thing for philosophical aesthetics.)

Now, as we have already noted, it can make a significant difference to an aesthetic response if it is known that what is being attended to is an artefact. For here, in contrast to natural phenomena, questions of meaning frequently arise (exceptions are objects such as rugs, pots, furniture, etc.). Even when what we call 'nature' bears obvious marks of human intervention, such marks are not characteristically to be 'read' as addressed to a spectator or a listener. Consider, for instance, a landscape studded with telegraph pylons, which might nevertheless be seen as 'elegant giantesses in long flimsy dresses strolling over the sturdy hills' (Sircello, 1975, p. 106). There is no need here for a knowledge of social or cultural contexts – though this is not to say that other sorts of knowledge might not be important for aesthetic enjoyment (as I shall discuss later), nor that someone familiar with the arts might not be influenced in his looking at and listening to sights and sounds of nature, and indeed find it difficult not to be so influenced (cf. Forge, 1973).

Imagination, then, has a certain scope in art that is not possible with natural objects. We have a certain freedom to interpret, for example, Pinter's *The Birthday Party* in the sense of construing it as a study of growing up, or of the pressures of bourgeois society on the artist, or as an allegory about death – or in other ways, perhaps (though all artistic appraisals are necessarily limited by both internal and external constraints). On the other hand, aesthetic appreciation of natural phenomena involves a certain freedom and certain opportunities of its own. For, as Hepburn points out, since they lack built-in guides and contextual controls such as an artist typically provides, and have no external devices such as pedestals or lighting that set off an art object from its environment, we are challenged to vary the boundaries of our attention and to integrate (or not, as we will) other sights and sounds into the overall experience.

Of course, features of a natural object or portion of the environment that are available to ordinary perception do, as with an art work, set limits to how we *interpret*, in the sense of whether we see it as stark, robust, or whatever. But we are none the less free to ignore, for example, a dark bank of cloud on the horizon so that the scene appears one of idyllic tranquillity, or to incorporate it so that the view takes on a menacing or exciting character. And so we may search, as Hepburn puts it, 'for ever new standpoints, and for more comprehensive *gestalts*' (op. cit., p. 15). Indeed, he claims that a task is thus set for our creativity; and though once again, as with the appreciation of an art work, it might be queried whether we can properly speak here of *creative* effort, many forms of the natural world offer abundant scope for aesthetic imagination, as he so tellingly illustrates.

Further, if the individual is in a forest, say, or ringed by hills or in the midst of a plain, his sense of his own being, Hepburn suggests, may be modified: as 'both actor and spectator, ingredient to the landscape', he may experience *himself* in an unusual and vivid way. This is also possible, however, within a building (as Hepburn mentions), or moving about among large pieces of sculpture; but it is more intense and pervasive in nature-experience, he maintains, since the person concerned is not only *in*, but also a *part of* nature. For some people, of course, experience of oneness with nature (of which Hepburn distinguishes various kinds) may go hand in hand with some forms of mysticism or with religious convictions; but even without a particular metaphysical viewpoint such as a belief in the 'artistry' of a Creator there can be no less a sense of wonderment and exhilaration if a leaf pattern is seen as chiming with a vein

## AESTHETIC EDUCATION OUTSIDE THE ARTS

pattern, 'cloud form with mountain form and mountain form with human form'. Nor need aesthetic experience of the natural world either involve the Wordsworthian belief in Nature as man's 'educator', conveying uplifting 'messages', or degenerate into the 'forced ecstasies and hypocrisies of a fashionable and trivialized nature-cult' (p. 9). It might nevertheless help to offset that sense of man as a stranger in the world, which is sometimes claimed to be this century's great problem of morale – the human being's feeling of not being at home on this planet, the malaise of alienation (see, for example, Sircello, 1975, ch. 1), but that dates back much earlier (as evident in German literature of the early nineteenth century, for example).

Some aesthetic experiences of natural phenomena, Hepburn further claims, involve the *realizing* of something, a coming-to-be-aware or a making vivid to perception and imagination (p. 27) – experience comparable, it might be suggested, to that sense of illumination sometimes gained in art, as discussed in the previous chapter. This, however, is not only overlooked in most of the literature of aesthetic education but is specifically denied in the APU document, where the claim that the arts 'can give increasing perceptiveness and insight about [*sic*] almost every aspect of life and the world around us' (para. 3.2) is not only altogether too strong but seriously misleading. For the arts are contrasted in this respect with the aesthetic: what constitutes the crucial difference between the two, it is asserted, is that there is nothing to be learned from the aesthetic!

I have already indicated that in this publication both the notion of learning in respect of the arts (which seems to be of the 'learning-that' kind) and the account of the aesthetic are highly problematic. But it is also worth considering other assumptions that may underlie such views in much of the literature of aesthetic education; and here another point briefly mentioned by Hepburn provides a clue. For he notes that an expression theory of art readily copes with artefacts, but not with natural objects. Riddled as so much educational thinking is with theories of expression and communication, it is perhaps little wonder that inquirers tend to turn away from considerations outside art and attribute more responsibility to it in this respect than it is able to bear.

Moreover, the education of feeling is conceived of almost

exclusively in terms of those feelings and emotions involved in social interaction and interpersonal understanding. Yet, important though these obviously are, it may be questioned whether pupils are to be presented with a view of the human condition without reference to the relationship of human beings to the natural world, including of course its animals. This clearly involves a powerful moral dimension, as evident in the now more widespread, if belated, concern for the natural environment; but it is sometimes also associated with, and might indeed arise from and be strengthened by an aesthetic interest in that environment.

Further, bearing in mind White's arguments for a curriculum which opens up knowledge of various life-styles not simply at the level of learning about, for example, how nomads live, but as regards the guiding principles which inform the choices individuals make, there would seem to be an important place for the gaining of some understanding of those patterns of life in which high value is placed on more solitary modes of existence and leisure pursuits – as, say, a lone yachtsman (or woman) or mountaineer. To make provision within education for aesthetic experience in relation to the natural world, however, may not be easy. For one thing, a measure of solitariness and comparative silence might be desirable, yet difficult to come by. Nor can one very well say, 'Now go off and have an aesthetic experience' (even in surroundings that seem favourable, and if what counts as 'aesthetic experience' is at least to some extent understood). Nevertheless, just as it is regarded as important by some schools for children to browse among books or pictures, so it should not be beyond the bounds of possibility – for instance, when they take part in expeditions to do with various kinds of studies – for pupils to spend some of the time, however short, simply looking and listening, perhaps alone, without any particular assignment; and educated, moreover, to find nothing strange in this.

At the very least, it seems only reasonable that there should be attempts to counterbalance some of the attitudes frequently fostered by those activities in which various aspects of the natural environment are regarded primarily as useful *targets* or *obstacles* against which to pit one's strength and physical skills or test one's capacity for survival – something to be assaulted, conquered and the like (ideas typically found, for example, in the literature of outdoor pursuits). This is not to say that such attitudes might not be part of a larger experience which includes an awareness of rocks, seas, caves, and so on, as, say, brooding, hostile or grim which could be aesthetic. It might even be claimed by some that attention can switch to and fro between the task in hand and appreciation of the surroundings as *beautiful*; yet in circumstances in which a primary concern is one's own prowess such an appraisal is not as easily achieved as many like to think.

There are perhaps numerous situations in which an aesthetic interest coincides, in experience, with some other interest. They might even reinforce each other, as for instance when particular forms of dress, music, dance, floral decorations and other aspects of an environment feature within a religious or civic or some other ceremony in such a way that, for some people, the total experience is more powerful than it would otherwise have been. But it might, as for example may happen in a school assembly, be correspondingly less so if, say, the music is aesthetically poor or badly performed. And problems all too easily arise, not least with children, when bodily movement is involved; for (as already noted in connection with dancing) pleasure in skilfulness or in the sensations of motion tends to threaten an aesthetic concern. Indeed, in his discussion of being in motion amid natural scenery, Hepburn is hardly correct in speaking of a glider pilot's delight in a sense of buoyancy as an element *within* his aesthetic experience; rather, it is additional to it. (One comes back again to the crucial point that aesthetic awareness is *educable*: what could one be brought to attend to with such sensations that might modify one's perceptions?)

Nevertheless, the possibility of aesthetic enjoyment arising in connection with the performing of some physical action or activity (that is, additionally) is not, as I have already indicated, arbitrarily to be ruled out, and is indeed strenuously argued for as one of the most valuable aspects of physical education by a number of writers on that subject, though the claims are sometimes exaggerated. Best (1978), however, has made a particularly valuable contribution here in distinguishing what he calls 'purposive' sports (the vast majority, such as ball games and athletics), where the aim can be specified independently of the manner of achieving it and where any aesthetic interest is thus purely incidental, and those he calls 'aesthetic' (such as diving, trampolining and figure-skating), where the aim is logically inseparable from the manner of achievement since considerations such as grace and effortlessness are taken into account – that is, they require judgement of *style*, not merely point-scoring according to set criteria. This second group, then, would appear to be of greater potential aesthetic value.

I shall not pursue further issues that arise in this connection as there is substantial literature on the subject within that of physical education/human movement studies, except to mention three points. First, it would seem desirable that, as in the arts, pupils should learn to participate in critical reflection and assessment and, moreover, might participate in this sense without having to take part in the event itself. Indeed, in all sports there can be connoisseurs who, like art connoisseurs, may have little skill (if any) as practitioners, but whose discrimination is not necessarily any poorer, and may in fact be a good deal sharper, than that of some expert performers.

Second (*pace* Best, 1978, p. 110; and cf. also my remarks in *Dance, Art and Aesthetics*, pp. 98ff.), a spectator who understands very little about, say, cricket may nevertheless enjoy the sheer beauty of some players' movements *out* of the context within which they occur (as distinct from their *moves* in the sense of manoeuvres or tactics, which clearly do require knowledge of the game to be appreciated aesthetically). Someone might, for instance, admire Dennis Lillee's run-up and bowling action from an aesthetic point of view, rather as he might a deer's running and leaping, while completely ignorant of the difference between bowling and throwing, let alone of the particular purpose of any single delivery (which even the most knowledgeable might find difficult to fathom until *after* the delivery of the ball).

Third, it perhaps needs to be emphasized that the quality of an athlete's performance in the 'purposive' sports is not a sufficient criterion of aesthetic satisfaction on his part. Certainly it is not to be separated from any such satisfaction that he does feel: as Best insists, his pleasure is not a distinct but perhaps concurrent activity. But, as with a workman, it is quite conceivable that the individual enjoys his achievement simply in terms of its efficiency, even if a spectator appreciates it aesthetically (nor need he, or anyone else, regard unsuccessful endeavours as aesthetic disasters). Even another cricketer, as Pole (1976) points out, might admire Clive Lloyd's supremely skilful strokes without any hint of aesthetic concern. In contrast, then, to decorating a cake or embroidering a dress, for example, which typically involves an aesthetic interest to be intelligible at all, something more is necessary to establish whether any pleasure experienced by a person who is engaged in some task has an aesthetic element. That is, some indication is needed of how he conceives of his performance. As with a spectator, he has to make it evident that his enjoyment has an imaginative dimension – that he regards the performance *as if* it were valuable simply as something to be looked at.

Once again, therefore, as with art works, what someone *says* about objects and performances outside art is of the utmost importance in the context of aesthetic education, and considerations discussed in the previous chapter as regards the need to build up appropriate and rich vocabularies apply here similarly. There might, indeed, seem to be a special challenge for aesthetic education outside the arts in this respect in as much as it is typically in connection with the countryside, gardens, the seaside and the like that 'beautiful,' 'lovely' and their cognates are widely – if often rather indiscriminately – used (think, for example, of holiday brochures and calendars of the 'Beautiful Britain' kind, or the remarks of many members of coach parties after only a casual, fleeting glance at their surroundings). Moreover, in the case of sport, working movements, machines and other objects skilfully designed for a purpose, such terms are often used to refer to their excellence as perfect specimens of their kind: all kinds of things, from burglaries to ulcers, may properly be described as *beautiful* purely in virtue of their perfection from this point of view (see, for example, De Quincey's amusing, but instructive essay 'On murder considered as one of the fine arts').

A problem in all this, however, is the dearth of appreciative texts, especially in connection with events and phenomena which of their very nature are transient or likely to be seen on other occasions under different conditions such as light, cloud formations, etc. Yet the situation is not much better in this respect than in the case of dance and radio and television productions. A great deal thus depends on the width and variety of experience and understanding on the part of teachers and parents. It is, of course, essential in aesthetic education outside no less than in the arts that progress be looked for and worked at, and that ways of expanding and deepening pupils' experience be sought rather than that they be exposed only to what may be generally accepted as aesthetically interesting but may involve little effort.

One consideration, once again, is the possible significance of certain information. Knowing, for example, something of how, over the centuries, the action of winds, ice, torrents, volcanic eruptions, etc., has brought about and continues to affect the shapes and forms of natural objects in all their astonishing diversity might heighten imaginative awareness of the rock formations of a glacial valley or the twisted pinnacles of a mountain ridge. Or, to take an example from Hepburn, one's experience of walking over a wide expanse of sand and mud may be modified if one learns that it is in fact a tidal basin and hence for half the day the sea-bed: the 'wild, glad emptiness' of the place may be tempered by a 'disturbing weirdness' (1966, p. 295).

Stereotyped responses might also be avoided and finer discriminations encouraged if, in outdoor situations especially, opportunities are given for pupils to encounter variety and complexity – beauty that is austere as well as lush, rugged as well as gentle, regular and trim as well as chaotic and wild; and if, further, they are helped to acquire habits of looking and listening such as shifting attention from one object to another and to spaces between objects, relating one detail to another and then to a wider context, or 'zooming in' on a tiny area rather than ranging over broad vistas.

Aesthetic appreciation of the environment, which might of course be a mixture of the natural and the man-made – skylines fretted by buildings, cranes or the tops of ships; railings and bridges silhouetted against water or grass, etc. – can obviously be linked with photography and film-making. But, as also with sketching or creative writing, for instance, the object or scene then becomes something to be *treated*, albeit from an artistic point of view. Interest necessarily centres on the standards and techniques appropriate to the activity in hand.

It may indeed be questioned whether, as claimed in *The Arts in Schools* (para. 73), 'the arts are the characteristic ways in which we record and reflect' upon experience such as that of looking at an insect's wing under a microscope, or at shells, fossils, plants, and so on. In the first place, as argued in earlier chapters, the arts do not record anything: in contrast to a botanist or a geologist or someone with a tape-recorder, an artist characteristically draws freely on his experience, using it as inspiration for a work of imagination. Second, individuals often want merely to 'stay' with the object or scene, especially if they lack sufficient skill to realize something of the experience in art-making. For children to be obliged, or at any rate expected, to engage in so-called creative activities following every visit or outing, every moving or unusual event or situation, may well ruin certain experiences.

Moreover, if painting and drawing are consistently limited to a particular kind of brush or pencil, surface or paint, looking can become correspondingly restricted; for the individual 'sees what he paints'. This might work to advantage in so far as it can be a means of selective and more intense focusing on the part of an artist who is already practised in the use of a range of materials and tools; but the less experienced person may require considerable practice before his looking can benefit from his painting, etc. Similarly with, as it were, bringing one's experience of certain art works to contemplation of the environment. Doubtless familiarity with particular poems, pieces of sculpture, paintings – even music – can result in one's attention being caught and held by certain aspects of things in such a way that, as Andrew Forge (1973) remarks, they 'blossom out' into something more resonant than the things themselves might seem to warrant. And since, far from there being 'innocent' eyes and ears, a great deal of our looking and listening is determined by other people's images – often, as in much advertising of the crude, glossy type – much is to be gained if pupils are sometimes enabled to perceive certain objects and scenes through the eyes and ears of artists who have communicated *their* impressions of (and with that, their responses to) similar objects and scenes in striking and subtle ways. Yet, again, if it is hoped that through such experience children may develop their own powers of looking at and listening to things outside art, familiarity with a *range* of art works in terms of differing styles and media is desirable.

However, habitually viewing scenes for their frame-worthiness, Hepburn (1984, p. 49) points out, can actually mar rather than enhance aesthetic awareness: as often as not, he claims, mentally putting them into a frame turns good natural beauty into mediocre quasi-art. And it would undoubtedly be a mistake to try to project onto natural phenomena the kind of formal unity, textures and colour harmonies that are to be found only in paintings (or, it might be added, sound qualities peculiar to music). More positively, there are subtle blends and gradations and vivid contrasts to be found in nature that are not to be found in art or other artefacts.

Teachers of the various arts are thus not the only, or necessarily the best, people to undertake aesthetic education outside the arts, though they would seem to have a rather greater responsibility than most in as much as they might be expected to be practised in aesthetic discussion in at least one art form and able to adapt accordingly. Certainly it is not to be supposed that, since the aesthetic may pervade every department of life, every teacher (or parent) is capable of engaging in the enterprise. The recommendation of *The Arts in Schools* that 'aesthetic experience, like creativity, should be fostered throughout the curriculum' (para. 73) is unquestionably far too simplistic. In any case, it can hardly be thought desirable that pupils should be encouraged to take an aesthetic interest in things whenever the opportunity presents itself. For there are many occasions on which this would be quite inappropriate: becoming absorbed in the patterns and colours of a graph, for instance, could result in failure to grasp the information it conveys; and taking a butterfly to pieces in order to enjoy the appearance of its wings in greater detail might justifiably be regarded as ethically objectionable.

Aesthetic preferences – or aesthetic indifference – may, of course be manifested by all teachers (and others) over a whole range of behaviour, from their hair-styles, what they wear and surround themselves with in their homes, to their speech and table 'manner(s)', their bodily carriage and gestures, and so forth. Moreover, it seems no accident that terms such as 'graceful' and 'clumsy' have application in the moral and psychological realms as well as the aesthetic. 'John rose to his feet awkwardly' may imply that John lacked inner composure as well as outward grace (Hepburn, 1984, p. 76). And although there are often many other factors operating here – income, fashion, social group, practicability, the desire to conform or to be different, etc. – such things may exert a powerful, if sometimes subtle, influence on young people. Yet even in cases of genuine aesthetic choice such preferences typically remain unexamined, and it can no more be claimed that all this contributes to aesthetic education than someone's frowning or shrugging his shoulders in certain circumstances can be thought to be an instance of moral education. If children merely *pick up* various attitudes, habits and practices unthinkingly, they are not learning to discriminate, to exercise personal judgement. The task has to be undertaken quite specifically.

Similarly with the appearance and care of the school building, its playground or garden and other surroundings. For unless attention is sometimes directed to particular features and critical appreciation fostered on the spot they are easily overlooked or come to be taken for granted. Indeed, an occasional walk around the premises with an aesthetically aware 'guide' might do more for aesthetic development than week after week of 'creative activities' with garish paint and paper, crumpled toilet-roll centres and battered tambourines, or the study of novels only from the point of view of their social and moral content, no matter what their literary quality. And not infrequently a 'lively and exciting' primary classroom in a modern building and 'stimulating' environment leaves as much to be desired aesthetically as the proverbially dark and drab games cupboard under the stairs in some old schools.

Ironically, in view of the continuing influence of some of the pioneers in education in the various arts of over a generation ago, much of what was admirable in their thinking has been largely neglected. Despite the inadequacy of his account of the aesthetic, and the many inconsistencies and contradictions in his writings on education, Read, for example – like Schiller – had a vision of aesthetic education that deserves serious reconsideration today. It is a vision in which, among other things, importance was accorded to beauty, grace and dignity – just those qualities that have tended to become downgraded in much art in recent decades and regarded as unfashionable subjects for discussion among a great many critics, philosophers and educationists alike. Yet numbers of people still seem to seek them, if sometimes in a rather groping, fumbling fashion, both within and outside the arts.

If 'aesthetic education' is to be more than a gaily paraded but virtually meaningless phrase, a great deal of further thought is required about the concept and about what can be done under this heading in schools and colleges that is both practicable and effective. This would seem especially urgent when a new utilitarianism is abroad in state education. But rather than holding their heads in their hands and following those who continue to mouth ever more platitudes and nonsense about the arts, creativity, and so forth, those who care have to tighten up their thinking and practice as regards not only their own special interests but also the claims of other subject areas within a general education. Not least, the education and training of teachers is in need of a radical overhaul in this connection, particularly as not a few practitioners seem often unprepared, or at any rate ill prepared, to examine rigorously precisely what they are doing, and why.

As well as becoming better equipped philosophically, however, teachers might be helped both to get their bearings and to counter (often well directed) criticism if they had a better understanding of the history of those ideas that are relevant to the aesthetic realm and of the ways in which they have featured in educational theory and practice in this century at least. For many of the questionable practices that are current today in connection with the arts and related areas derive from ideas that were perhaps refreshing, if sometimes rather naïve, fifty years ago, but that have hardened into dogma instead of being constantly reviewed and adapted, as necessary, so that they may contribute to an education that is, literally, progressive.

# Further Reading

A major difficulty besets the student or teacher eager to pursue his philosophical studies in relation to aesthetic education, namely the dearth not only of suitable texts but of virtually any texts that are devoted specifically to the topic as a whole. Even if the subject is restricted to aesthetic education in the arts, comparatively little high-class literature by British authors is available, and while there is now a considerable amount of work published in the United States it is apt to be variable in quality and, again, focuses overwhelmingly on the fine arts. With this qualification, however, the *Journal of Aesthetic Education* may be highly recommended (Britain has no comparable publication). The collection by R. A. Smith, *Aesthetic Concepts and Education* (Urbana, Ill.: University of Illinois Press, 1970), and that of G. Pappas, *Concepts in Art and Education* (London: Collier-Macmillan, 1970), also remain useful, though published well over a decade ago.

With these considerations in mind, I have laced the present text with quotations and references in an attempt both to give a 'flavour' of the author in question and to signpost where the reader might go to follow up particular points in more detail.

A further difficulty is that reading can usually proceed profitably in this area only against the background of an acquaintance with general aesthetics, which in turn cannot be achieved in isolation, but requires some grasp of metaphysics, of ethics, epistemology, philosophy of mind, and of logic (though not in the narrow sense of rules of inference, but in the broader sense of the study of principles of reasoning and valid argument). It has, indeed, to be acknowledged that aesthetic problems are among some of the most teasing and often seemingly intractable in the whole of philosophy, and it is therefore hardly surprising that much of the best work tends to be tough going. Recent publications in particular, making up lost ground in terms of a lack of stringency in much writing on aesthetics and the arts in the first half of the century, can be daunting to the philosophically unsophisticated reader, and one therefore may have to be content at first with taking what one can from part of a chapter, a paper, or even a few paragraphs, and then returning at a later stage. (A good example here is the work of Scruton, already referred to, which, however, amply rewards persistent application.)

Moreover, what may be styled an introduction to aesthetics is often not introductory at all in the sense of being intended for the beginner in philosophy. Wollheim's *Art and Its Objects* is a case in point – but again well worth the effort. The extensive references for each section have been updated in the second edition (1980), which also has the advantage of an outline of the argument as well as six supplementary essays (no less demanding!).

Probably still the best genuine introduction is Ruth Saw's (1972), mentioned in the text; but a more recent welcome addition that is in effect an introductory text is H. Gene Blocker's *Philosophy of Art* (New York: Charles Scribner's Sons, 1979). Somewhere in between the two extremes is William Charlton's *Aesthetics: An Introduction* (London: Hutchinson, 1970), which has a particularly valuable opening chapter on aesthetics and philosophy. Jerome Stolnitz's short *Aesthetics* (New York: Macmillan, 1965), is relatively easy reading, while his longer and more advanced *Aesthetics and Philosophy of Art Criticism* (Boston, Mass.: Houghton & Mifflin, 1960), along with F. E. Sparshott's *The Structure of Aesthetics* (London: Routledge & Kegan Paul, 1963), his *The Concept of Criticism* (Oxford: OUP, 1967) and Margolis's *The Language of Art and Art Criticism* (Detroit: Wayne State University Press, 1965) are useful guides in the critical realm. V. C. Aldrich's *Philosophy of Art* (Englewood Cliffs, N.J.: Prentice-Hall, 1963) and Harold Osborne's *The Art of Appreciation* (London: OUP, 1970) are also readily accessible to the general reader.

The two major journals in the field, *The British Journal of Aesthetics* and the American *Journal of Aesthetics and Art Criticism* are especially valuable in terms both of variety of subject-matter and of range of difficulty, and sometimes include papers which bear on aesthetic education, as well as reviews of writings by educationists in the sphere of the arts. In addition, the *Journal of the History of Ideas* deserves to be better known to students of the arts and aesthetics than it generally would appear to be.

Many anthologies of aesthetic writings exist (though there are numerous overlaps of material), and readers may find these helpful in as much as, according to their particular interests and stage of philosophical development, they may find certain pieces of greater appeal than others and then be able to move on to others. Osborne's *Aesthetics* (London: OUP, 1972) provides a comprehensive account of, as it were, the state of aesthetic inquiry as it stood in 1972, and also has a most useful bibliography, including a section devoted exclusively to music. Recent additions to collected writings on aesthetics, somewhat more difficult on the whole than former anthologies, are B. R. Tilghman's *Language and Aesthetics* (Kansas: Kansas University Press,

1973) and E. H. Coleman's *Varieties of Aesthetic Experience* (Washington, DC: University Press of America, 1983).

Earlier 'classics' which are perhaps best read when one's critical powers have been sharpened up include Bell's *Art* (1914), R. G. Collingwood's *The Principles of Art* (Oxford: OUP, 1938), B. Croce's [1901] *Aesthetics* (London: Macmillan, 1922 edition), Tolstoy's *What is Art?* [1899] (London: OUP, 1930 edition), and John Dewey's *Art as Experience* (London: Putnam, 1934).

No bibliographical essay on aesthetics would be complete without mention of Immanuel Kant's *Critique of Judgment*, the foundation stone of modern aesthetics. But this presents immense problems – and not only for the beginner. For one thing there is, as yet, no satisfactory English translation (there is little to choose between Bernard's and Meredith's). Furthermore it has to be seen within the context of Kant's work as a whole and in particular presupposes the argument of the *Critique of Pure Reason*'s Transcendental Analytic. Nevertheless, within the last decade or so a number of Kant scholars have opened up that part of the *Critique of Judgment*, the Critique of Aesthetic Judgment, which would seem of greatest value to readers wishing to attempt an excursion into this extremely difficult field, and have made abundantly clear its central relevance for contemporary aesthetic inquiry. D. W. Crawford's *Kant's Aesthetic Theory* (Wisconsin: Wisconsin University Press, 1974) is perhaps the most easily readable, but outstanding contributions are Paul Guyer's *Kant and the Claims of Taste* (Cambridge, Mass.: Harvard University Press, 1979) and the collection edited by Ted Cohen and Paul Guyer, *Essays on Kant's Aesthetics* (Chicago: Chicago University Press, 1982). Eva Schaper's six essays, *Studies in Kant's Aesthetics* (1979), which are referred to in the text, are also useful and include one on Schiller in relation to Kant. It is strongly recommended, however, that all such reading be pursued under the guidance of a professional philosopher.

# References

Bantock, G. H. (1971), 'Towards a theory of popular education', in *The Curriculum: Context and Development*, ed. R. Hooper (Edinburgh: Oliver & Boyd), pp. 251–64.
Baxter, B. (1983), 'Conventions and art', *British Journal of Aesthetics*, vol. 23, no. 4, pp. 319–32.
Beardsley, M. C. (1958), *Aesthetics: Problems in the Philosophy of Criticism* (New York: Harcourt, Brace & World).
Beardsmore, R. W. (1973), 'Two trends in contemporary aesthetics', *British Journal of Aesthetics*, vol. 13, no. 4, pp. 346–66.
Bell, C. (1931), *Art* [1914] (London: Chatto & Windus).
Best, D. (1974), *Expression in Movement and the Arts* (London: Lepus Books, Henry Kimpton).
Best, D. (1978), *Philosophy and Human Movement* (London: Allen & Unwin).
Best, D. (1979), 'Free expression, or the teaching of techniques?', *British Journal of Educational Studies*, vol. 27, no. 3, pp. 210–20.
Binkley, T. (1976), 'Deciding about art', in *Culture and Art*, ed. L. Aagaard-Mogensen (Atlantic Highlands, NJ: Humanities Press), pp. 90–109.
Binkley, T. (1978), 'Piece: contra aesthetics', in *Philosophy Looks at the Arts* (2nd edn), ed. J. Margolis (Philadelphia, Pa, Philadelphia University Press), pp. 25–44.
Broudy, H. (1972), *Englightened Cherishing: An Essay in Aesthetic Education* (Urbana, Ill.: University of Illinois Press).
Calouste Gulbenkian Foundation (1980), *Dance Education and Training in Britain* (London: Calouste Gulbenkian Foundation).
Calouste Gulbenkian Foundation (1982), *The Arts in Schools: Principles, Practice and Provision* (London: Calouste Gulbenkian Foundation).
Cameron, J. M. (1962), *The Night Battle* (London: Burns & Oates).
Casey, J. (1973), 'The autonomy of art', in *Philosophy and the Arts*, Royal Institute of Philosophy Lectures, Vol. 6 (London: Macmillan), pp. 65–87.
Charlton, W. (1972), 'Aestheticism', *British Journal of Aesthetics*, vol. 12, no. 2, pp. 121–32.
Cohen, M. (1965), 'Aesthetic essence', in *Philosophy in America*, ed. M. Black (London: Allen & Unwin), pp. 115–33.
Cohen, T. (1983), 'Jokes', in *Pleasure, Preference and Value*, ed. E. Schaper (Cambridge: CUP), pp. 120–36.
Coleridge, S. T. (1956), *Biographia Literaria* [1817] (London: Dent).
Collinson, D. (1973), 'Aesthetic education', in *New Essays in the Philosophy of Education*, ed. G. Langford and D. J. O'Connor (London: Routledge & Kegan Paul), pp. 197–215.

# REFERENCES

Crowther Report, Central Advisory Council for Education (1959), *15-18* (London: HMSO).
Danto, A. (1973), 'Artworks and real things', *Theoria*, vol. 39, no. 1, pp. 1–17.
Danto, A. (1978), 'The artworld' [1964], in *Philosophy Looks at the Arts* (2nd edn), ed. J. Margolis (Philadelphia, Pa: Philadelphia University Press), pp. 132–44.
Department of Education and Science (1972), *Movement: Physical Education in the Primary Years* (London: HMSO).
Department of Education and Science (1977), *Curriculum 11–16, Working Papers by HM Inspectorate: A Contribution to Current Debate* (London: HMSO).
Department of Education and Science (1978), *Primary Education in England* (London: HMSO).
Department of Education and Science (1982a), *Education 5–9: An Illustrative Survey of 80 First Schools in England* (London: HMSO).
Department of Education and Science (1982b), *Aesthetic Development* (London: HMSO).
Diblasio, M. K. (1983), 'The troublesome concept of child art: a threefold analysis', *Journal of Aesthetic Education*, vol. 17, no. 3, pp. 71–84.
Dickie, G. (1969), 'The myth of the aesthetic attitude' [1964] in *Introductory Readings in Aesthetics*, ed. J. Hospers (New York: Macmillan), pp. 28–45.
Dickie, G. (1971), *Aesthetics: An Introduction* (New York: Pegasus Press).
Dickie, G. (1974), *Art and the Aesthetic: An Institutional Analysis* (New York: Cornell University Press).
Dickie, G. (1976), 'What is art?', in *Culture and Art*, ed. L. Aagaard-Mogensen (Atlantic Highlands, NJ: Humanities Press), pp. 21–31.
Diffey, T. J. (1973), 'Essentialism and the definition of "art" ', *British Journal of Aesthetics*, vol. 13, no. 2, pp. 103–20.
Diffey, T. J. (1979), 'On defining art', *British Journal of Aesthetics*, vol. 19, no. 1, pp. 16–23.
Elliott, R. K. (1971), 'Versions of creativity', *Proceedings of the Philosophy of Education Society of Great Britain*, vol. V, no. 2, pp. 139–52.
Elliott, R. K. (1972) 'The critic and the lover of art', in *Linguistic Analysis and Phenomenology*, ed. W. Mays and S. C. Brown (London: Macmillan), pp. 118–27.
Elliott, R. K. (1974), 'Education, love of one's subject and the love of truth', *Proceedings of the Philosophy of Education Society of Great Britain*, vol. 8, no. 1, pp. 135-53.
Foreman-Peck, L. (1983), 'Learning from literature', *Journal of Aesthetic Education*, vol. 17, no. 3, pp. 57–69.
Forge, A. (1973), 'Art/Nature', in *Philosophy and the Arts*, Royal Institute of Philosophy Lectures, Vol. 6 (London: Macmillan), pp. 228–41.
Foster, A. W. (1976), 'The slow radical: restrictions on the artist as a change agent', *British Journal of Aesthetics*, vol. 16, no. 2, pp. 161–9.
Furlong, E. J. (1961), *Imagination* (London: Allen & Unwin).
Gallie, W. B. (1964), *Philosophy and the Historical Understanding* (London: Chatto & Windus).

Gombrich, E. H. (1960), *Art and Illusion* (London: Phaidon Press).
Goodman, N. (1968), *Languages of Art* (London: OUP).
Hartnett, A., and Naish, M. (1976), *Theory and the Practice of Education*, Vol. 1 (London: Routledge & Kegan Paul).
Hepburn, R. W. (1966), 'Contemporary aesthetics and the neglect of natural beauty', in *British Analytical Philosophy*, ed. B. Williams and A. Montefiore (London: Routledge & Kegan Paul), pp. 286–309.
Hepburn, R. W. (1972), 'The arts and the education of feeling and emotion', in *Education and the Development of Reason*, ed. R. F. Dearden, P. H. Hirst and R. S. Peters (London: Routledge & Kegan Paul), pp. 484–500.
Hepburn, R. W. (1984), *'Wonder' and Other Essays: Eight Studies in Aesthetics and Neighbouring Fields* (Edinburgh: Edinburgh University Press). This includes the essay cited above.
Hirst, P. H. (1974), *Knowledge and the Curriculum* (London: Routledge & Kegan Paul).
Hirst, P. H., and Peters, R. S. (1970), *The Logic of Education* (London: Routledge & Kegan Paul).
Holt, M. (1978), *The Common Curriculum: Its Structure and Style in the Comprehensive School* (London: Routledge & Kegan Paul).
Hospers, J. (1946), *Meaning and Truth in the Arts* (Chapel Hill, NC: University of North Carolina Press).
Hungerland, I. C. (1972), 'Once again, aesthetic and non-aesthetic', [1968], in *Aesthetics*, ed. H. Osborne (London: OUP), pp. 106–20.
Johnson, R. V. (1969), *Aestheticism* (London: Methuen).
Kant, I. (1933), *Critique of Pure Reason* [1781], translated N. Kemp Smith (London: Macmillan).
Kant, I. (1972), *Critique of Judgment* [1790], translated J. H. Bernard (New York: Hafner).
Kennick, W. E. (1965), 'Does traditional aesthetics rest on a mistake?' [1965], in *Collected Papers on Aesthetics*, ed. C. Barrett (Oxford: Blackwell), pp. 1–21.
Laban, R. (1963), *Modern Educational Dance* [1948] (2nd edn, revised L. Ullmann) (London: Macdonald & Evans).
Langer, S. K. (1953), *Feeling and Form* (London: Routledge & Kegan Paul).
Langer, S. K. (1957), *Problems of Art* (London: Routledge & Kegan Paul).
Meager, R. (1965), 'The uniqueness of a work of art' [1958], in *Collected Papers on Aesthetics*, ed. C. Barrett (Oxford: Blackwell), pp. 23–45.
Meager, R. (1970), 'Aesthetic concepts', *British Journal of Aesthetics*, vol. 10, no. 4, pp. 303–22.
Meager, R. (1974), 'Art and beauty', *British Journal of Aesthetics*, vol. 14, no. 2, pp. 99–105.
Meeson, P. (1972), 'Drawing, art and education', *British Journal of Aesthetics*, vol. 12, no. 3, pp. 276–89.
Meeson, P. (1981), review of *The Teaching Process and Arts and Aesthetics* (ed. G. L. Knieter and J. Stallings), *British Journal of Aesthetics*, vol. 21, no. 2, pp. 180–2.
Morris-Jones, H. (1968), 'The language of feelings' [1962], in *Aesthetics in the Modern World*, ed. H. Osborne (London: Thames & Hudson), pp. 94–104.

# REFERENCES

Murdoch, I. (1970), *The Sovereignty of Good* (London: Routledge & Kegan Paul).
Oakeshott, M. )1967), 'Learning and teaching', in *The Concept of Education*, ed. R. S. Peters (London: Routledge & Kegan Paul), pp. 156–76.
O'Connor, D. J. (1982), 'Two concepts of education', *Journal of the Philosophy of Education Society of Great Britain*, vol. 16, no. 2, pp. 137–46.
Osborne, H. (1952), *Theory of Beauty* (London: Routledge & Kegan Paul).
Osborne, H. (1968), *Aesthetics and Art Theory* (London: Longman).
Pevsner, N. (1945), *The Leaves of Southwell* (Harmondsworth: Penguin).
Phenix, P. H. (1964), *Realms of Meaning* (New York: McGraw-Hill).
Pole, D. (1976), 'Art, imagination and Mr. Scruton', *British Journal of Aesthetics*, vol. 16, no. 3, pp. 195–209.
Read, H. (1943), *Education Through Art* (London: Faber).
Redfern, H. B. (1976), 'Rudolf Laban and the aesthetics of dance', *British Journal of Aesthetics*, vol. 16, no. 1, pp. 61–7.
Redfern, H. B. (1982), *Concepts in Modern Educational Dance* [1972] (London: Dance Books Ltd).
Redfern, H. B. (1983), *Dance, Art and Aesthetics* (London: Dance Books Ltd).
Redfern, H. B. (1984), 'The place and use of language in dance appreciation', NATFHE Dance Section's *Collected Papers in Dance*, vol. 3, pp. 1–12.
Reid, L. A. (1961), *Ways of Knowledge and Experience* (London: Allen & Unwin).
Reid, L. A. (1969), *Meaning in the Arts* (London: Allen & Unwin).
Reid, L. A. (1970), 'Feeling and understanding', in *Aesthetic Concepts and Education*, ed. R. A. Smith (Urbana, Ill.: University of Illinois Press), pp. 45–76.
Reid, L. A. (1973), 'Knowledge, aesthetic insight and education', *Proceedings of the Philosophy of Education Society of Great Britain*, vol. 7, no. 1, pp. 66–84.
Rogers, L. R. (1968), 'Sculptural thinking' [1963], in *Aesthetics in the Modern World*, ed. H. Osborne (London: Thames & Hudson), pp. 197–208 and 215–21.
Rogers, L. R. (1969), *Sculpture* (London: OUP).
Rosebury, B. J. (1979), 'Fiction, emotion and "belief": a reply to Eva Schaper', *British Journal of Aesthetics*, vol. 19, no. 2, pp. 120–30.
Saw, R. (1972), *Aesthetics: An Introduction* (London: Macmillan).
Schaper, E. (1968), *Prelude to Aesthetics* (London: Allen & Unwin).
Schaper, E. (1972), Chairman's remarks 'The critic and the lover of art', in *Linguistic Analysis and Phenomenology*, ed. W. Mays and S. C. Brown (London: Macmillan), pp. 137–44.
Schaper, E. (1978), 'Fiction and the suspension of disbelief', *British Journal of Aesthetics*, vol. 18, no. 1, pp. 31–44.
Schaper, E. (1979), *Studies in Kant's Aesthetics* (Edinburgh: Edinburgh University Press).
Schaper, E. (1985), 'Towards the aesthetic: a journey with Friedrich Schiller', *British Journal of Aesthetics*, vol. 25, no. 2, pp. 153–68.
Schiller, J. C. F. (1967), *On the Aesthetic Education of Man – in a Series of Letters* [1801], translated and ed. E. M. Wilkinson and L. A. Willoughby (Oxford: Clarendon Press).

Scruton, R. (1974), *Art and Imagination* (London: Methuen).
Scruton, R. (1979), *The Aesthetics of Architecture* (London: Methuen).
Scruton, R. (1983), *The Aesthetic Understanding* (London: Methuen).
Sibley, F. N. (1965), 'Aesthetic concepts' [1959], in *Collected Papers on Aesthetics*, ed. C. Barrett (Oxford: Blackwell), pp. 61–89.
Sibley, F. N. (1974), 'Particularity, art and evaluation', *Aristotelian Society*, suppl. vol. 48, pp. 1–21.
Simpson, A. (1983), 'The concept of aesthetic education in Britain', *Journal of Aesthetic Education*, vol. 16, no. 3, pp. 35–47.
Sircello, G. (1972), *Mind and Art: An Essay on the Varieties of Expression* (Princeton, NJ: Princeton University Press).
Sircello, G. (1975), *A New Theory of Beauty* (Princeton, NJ: Princeton University Press).
Stevenson, C. L. (1963), *Facts and Values: Studies in Ethical Analysis* [1938] (New Haven, Conn.: Yale University Press).
Strawson, P. F. (1974), 'Aesthetic appraisal and works of art' [1953], in his *Freedom and Resentment and other essays* (London: Methuen), pp. 178–88.
Symes, C. (1983), 'Creativity: a divergent point of view', *Journal of Aesthetic Education*, vol. 17, no. 2, pp. 83–96.
Tormey, A. (1971), *The Concept of Expression: A Study in Philosophical Psychology and Aesthetics* (Princeton, NJ: Princeton University Press).
Urmson, J. O. (1962), 'What makes a situation aesthetic?' [1957], in *Philosophy Looks at the Arts*, ed. J. Margolis (New York: Scribner's Sons), pp. 13–27.
Weitz, M. (1978), 'The role of theory in aesthetics' [1956], in *Philosophy Looks at the Arts* (2nd edn), ed. J. Margolis (Philadelphia, Pa: University Press), pp. 121–31. (Also published in the 1st edn.)
Weston, M. (1975), 'How can we be moved by the fate of Anna Karenina?', *Aristotelian Society*, suppl. vol. 49, pp. 81–93.
White, J. P. (1972), 'Creativity and education: a philosophical analysis' [1968], in *Education and the Development of Reason*, ed. R. F. Dearden, P. H. Hirst and R. S. Peters (London: Routledge & Kegan Paul), pp. 132–48.
White, J. P. (1973), *Towards a Compulsory Curriculum* (London: Routledge & Kegan Paul).
Wigman, M. (1966), *The Language of Dance* (London: Macdonald & Evans).
Wilson, J. (1978), 'Education and aesthetic appreciation', in *Growing up with Philosophy*, ed. M. Lipman and A. M. Sharp (Philadelphia, Pa: Temple University), pp. 301–11.
Wittgenstein, L. (1953), *Philosophical Investigations*, translated G. E. M. Anscombe (Oxford: Blackwell).
Wittgenstein, L. (1966), *Lectures and Conversations on Aesthetics, Psychology and Religious Belief*, ed. C. Barrett (Oxford: Blackwell).
Wittgenstein, L. (1967) *Zettel*, translated G. E. M. Anscombe, ed. G. E. M. Anscombe and G. H. von Wright (Oxford: Blackwell).
Wollheim, R. (1968), *Art and Its Objects: An Introduction to Aesthetics* (London: Harper & Row).
Wollheim, R. (1973), *On Art and the Mind* (London: Allen Lane).

# Index

academic studies 70, 71
*Advent* (Coffey) 55
'aesthetic' 1, 13, 14, 70
aesthetic, accounts of the Ch. 2 *passim*, 89, 101, 109–10
  concept of the 1, 4, 13, Ch. 2 *passim*, 71
aesthetic appraisals (judgements), justification of 12, 61–5, 68, 92, 96, 97
  appreciation and art, 1, 4, Ch. 2, 67, 98–100, 101
    of the environment (see also 'aesthetics of everyday life') 4, Ch. 6 *passim*
    of nature 3, 17, 28–9, Ch. 6 *passim*
  attitude (standpoint) 4, 19ff., Chs. 4, 5, 6 *passim*
  awareness and affective response (see also feeling) 17, 19, 45, 83
    and animals 41–2, 102
    and imagination 18, 22, 23, Ch. 4 *passim*, 100, 101, 105
    and intellectual effort (see also thinking) 50
    and moral awareness (appraisal) 4, 5, 9, 10, 23, 37, 65, 66, 76, 102, 109
    and scientific awareness 5, 49–50
    and understanding persons 60, 86–7, 90, 96
  concepts, 5, 19–21, 95–6
  criteria (see also standards) 11, 61ff.
  development 11, 45–6, 68, 76–7, 85ff., 109
  distance, distancing 57–9, 93
  emotion 54
  features, qualities 5, 18–21, 23, 91
  feeling 53–8
  perception Ch. 2 *passim*, 47, 81, 90–1, 96, 101
  remarks 53
  use of words 19–21, 91
'aesthetic and creative' 5–6, 12
*Aesthetic Development* (DES) (*see also* APU document) 4, 7

aesthetic education, concept of 1, 9, 12, 20, 29, 110
aestheticism 4, 17–18
aesthetics 14, 17, 99, 111–13
'aeesethetics of everyday life' (*see also* aesthetic appreciation of the environment) 4
aim(s) 9–10, 75, 94
alienation 101
André, Carl 31
anthologies 86, 87
'appreciation' 7–8, 11
APU document (*Aesthetic Development*) (DES) 4, 7, 18, 61, 71, 85, 97, 98, 101
architecture (*see also* buildings) 7, 31, 78, 91, 95
Arden, J. 7
Aristotle 16
'art' 33
art(s) and the aesthetic 1, 4, Ch. 2 *passim*, 67, 98–100, 101
  and animals 40ff.
  and children 30, 36, 39ff., Chs. 5, 6 *passim*
  and craft(s) 2, 31
  and education Ch. 1 *passim*, 29–30, 39, 42–5, 60ff., Ch. 5, 97, 98, 99, 101, 107, 109, 110
  and life 23, 56–7, 101
  and moral development, morality 9, 10, 23, 37, 76
  and persons 60, 86–7, 90, 96
  and society 35–8
  and tradition(s) 36, 41, 43, 81, 82, 98
  as language(s) 8, 81–2
  concept of 11, 13, Ch. 2 *passim*, Ch. 3, 71, 79, 95, 96
  conventions in 36, 37, 51, 59, 81, 82, 83
  criteria of excellence in (see also rules, standards) 11, 31
criticism 14–15, 62, 78
fine 16, 17, 31, 105

art(s) and the aesthetic—*cont.*
  history of, historical perspective in 6, 27–8, 29, 35
  kinetic 36
  media, medium 40, 74, 78, 82, 108
  non-verbal 70
  performing 6, 68, 87
  philosophy of 14–15
  popular 76, 89
  post-modern 25–8, 29
  socio-historical character of 35ff., 82
  theories, theory of 29, Ch. 3 *passim*, 80, 82
  three-dimensional 91
  visual 2, 8, 17, 98
  works, works of art 17, 25, Ch. 3 *passim*, 54, 57, Ch. 5 *passim*, 97, 100, 105, 107, 108
'art for art's sake' 17
'art of movement' 71
artist(s) 4, 26, 32, 35, 38, 40–1, 43, 51, 56, 59, Ch. 5 *passim*, 100, 117
*Arts in Schools, The* (Gulbenkian Foundation) 5, 7, 8, 21, 71–2, 74, 80, 83, 85, 107, 108
artworld 35, 36
*as if* 21, 105
assessment (*see also* checking, evaluation) 10, 61
  self- 76, 94
attention 19, 23, Ch. 4 *passim*, 67, 103, 106, 107, 109

Bacon, F. 57
ballet
  jazz 36
  Romantic classical 39
Bantock, G. H. 70
Baumgarten, A. 13, 16, 17
Baxter, B. 81
Beardsley, M. C. 20
Beardsmore, R. 28–9
beauty, the beautiful 4, 16–19, 29, 31, 47, 67, 86, 99, 103, 104, 108, 110
'beauty', 'beautiful' 19, 33, 67, 105
Beckett, S. 7
Beethoven, L. van 95
belief(s) 40ff., Ch. 4 *passim*
believe, believing Ch. 4 *passim*
Bell, C. 32, 54
Best, D. 82, 83, 84, 103–4
Binkley, T. 25
birdsong 31, 40

*Birthday Party, The* (Pinter) 99
Bolt, R. 7
Botticelli, S. 68
Britten, B. 30
Brooke, R. 3
Broudy, H. 90
building(s) (*see also* architecture) 100, 106
  school 4, 109
*Byzantium* (Yeats) 89

Cage, J. 28
Calder, A. 62
Cameron, J. M. 85
Casey, J. 85, 87
cause(s), contrasted with reasons 53, 54
Charlton, W. 23
checking aesthetic understanding (*see also* assessment) 87ff.
'child art' 30, 42–4
children and aesthetic interest 23, 28, 30, 67, Ch. 5 *passim*, Ch. 6 *passim*
  and art 30, 36, 39ff., Ch. 5 *passim*
  'less able' 8
'children of bronze' 70
choice(s), choosing 40, 98, 102, 109
cinema 7, 36, 95
clothes (*see also* dress) 46
Coffey, B. 55
cognition 50
Cohen, T. 23, 64
Coleridge, S. T. 9, 49
Collingwood, R. G. 14
Collinson, D. 57, 87, 89, 90, 92
communication 8, 68, 80ff., 101
  theory of art 80–3
comparison(s) 88, 89, 93
compulsory (common) curriculum 5, 8, 10, 12, 95
concept(s) 11, 12, 20, 21, 25, 38, 48, 49, 91, 95
  acquiring 36, 38, 42, 48
  aesthetic 5, 19
  'essentially complex and essentially contested' 33, 43
  non-aesthetic 5
'configurational coherence' 60
Constable, J. 96
contemplation 21–2, 23, 67
context(s) 20, 32, 35, 48, 58, 61, 64, 86, 99, 104
contrast(s) 89, 93, 108
convention(s) 36, 37, 51, 59, 81, 82, 83
craft(s) 2, 3, 6, 31, 62, 97, 98

# INDEX

craftsmanship (*see also* skill, skilfulness) 15, 91
creative activity, activities 5–6, 8, 44, 59, 65, 72, 75, 94, 95, 107, 109
'creative arts, the' 6
creativity 9, 11, 43, Ch. 5 *passim*, 100, 108, 110
 concept of 5, 68, 69, 70ff.
critic(s) 4, 38, 62, 90, 92, 110
criticism 14–15, 62, 78
 self- 94
Crowther Report *15–18*, 69
*Curriculum 11–16* (DES) 1, 2, 3, 4, 5, 6, 18, 81, 83, 97

Dance, dancing 2, 5, 10, 36, 37, 68, 70, 72, 75, 79, 82, 91, 92, 95, 103, 106
 gestures 59
 ice- 31
*Dance Education* (Gulbenkian Report) 9, 69, 82, 93
Danto, A. 27, 35
Day Lewis, C. 86
defining, definition(s) 31–3, 35, 38, 82
 persuasive 33, 82
 ostensive 38
delight (*see also* enjoyment, pleasure, satisfaction) 3, 54, 57
De Quincey, T. 105
design and technology 3, 9, 97
desire(s) 22, 53, 66
development 3, 9–10, 43
 aesthetic 11, 45–6, 68, 76–7, 85ff., 109
 artistic 68, 76–7, 85ff.
 human 43, 80
 moral 9–10, 76
 social (*see also* understanding) 9
Diblasio, M. K. 43
Dickie, G. 23, 28, 35
Diffey, T. J. 28, 34, 39
discussion 6–7, 89ff., 108
disinterestedness 15, 22
distance, distancing 57–9, 93
Douglas, K. 64
*Dr. Faustus* (Marlowe) 57
drama (*see also* plays) 2, 5, 6, 7, 10
drawing 2, 5, 43, 75, 107
dress (*see also* clothes) 3, 17, 67, 98, 103
Duchamp, M. 28
*Duchess of Malfi, The* 86

*East Coker* (Eliot) 84

education, concept of 33
 and the arts Ch. 1 *passim*, 29–30, 39, 42–5, 60ff., Ch. 5, 97, 98, 99, 101, 107, 109, 110
 of emotions (*see also* feeling) 9
 of feeling 68, 85–6, 95, 101–2
 moral (*see also* development) 9, 66
*Education 5–9* (DES) 2, 6–7
Eliot, T. S. 56, 68, 84, 90
Elliott, R. K. 5, 21, 71, 85, 92
emotion(s) (*see also* feeling(s)) 17, 32, 53, 54, 57, 69, 79, 83, 84, 102
 aesthetic 54
 education of (*see also* feeling) 9
 and intellect 69–70
enjoyment (*see also* delight, pleasure, satisfaction) 10, 22, 42, 53, 56, 75, 76
 participant and spectator 73
entertaining a thought (*see also* supposing) 46, 49, 52
environment(s) Ch. 6 *passim*
'ethics' 14
evaluation (*see also* assessment) 15, 62
evaluative character of aesthetic appraisal 19
 use of terms 39
*Evita* (Rice and Webber) 30
experiencing as (*see also* hearing as, seeing as) 49, 50–2
expression 8, 32, 68, 69, 70, 77ff. 95
 'free' 83
 self- 80
 theories of art 80ff., 101
Expressionism 80
'expressive arts, the' 6
expressiveness 77ff.
 and animals 41

family resemblance(s) 33–4
fantasy 9, 22, 58, 65–6, 75
feeling(s) 8, 17, 18, 20, 32, 38, Ch. 4 *passim*, 99
 aesthetic 53–8
 education of 68, 85–6, 95, 101–2
fiction 25, 31, 56
film(s) (*see also* cinema) 63–4
 -making 106
first-order features, properties 46–7, 51, 52, 60
*Fish* (Hughes) 89
'for its (their) own sake' 22, 23, 27, 55, 66
Foreman-Peck, L. 56
Forge, A. 99, 107

form(s) 23, 24, 31, 32, 58–61, 66, 76–7, 88
'form of life' 35
Foster, A. 37
*Four Quartets* (Eliot) 68
freedom 33, 48, 49, 95, 99–100
  in aesthetic experience 19, 56
  in art 56, 79, 81, 95, 99–100
  of expression 43, 70, 83
Frye, N. 68
Furlong, E. J. 46

Gallie, W. B. 33, 35
game(s) 34, 104
gardens 2, 7, 31, 105, 109
Gill, E. 73
Gombrich, E. H. 43
Goodman, N. 27
Graham, M. 94

*Hamlet* (Shakespeare) 57
'harmonisation' 70
Hartnett, A. 33
*Haywain, The* (Constable) 96
hearing as (*see also* experiencing as) 46, 50, 51, 56
Hepburn, R. W. 59, 88, 89, 98–101, 103, 106, 108, 109
Hepworth, B. 40
Hirst, P. H. 25
history of art 27–8, 29, 35
  of ideas 11, 110
Holt, M. 6
home economics 97
Hospers, J. 65
Hughes, T. 89
Hungerland, I. C. 20

imaging (see also mental images) 46, 47, 52
imagination, 7, 8, 11, 18, 22, 23, 25, 27, 32, 43, Ch. 4 *passim*, 69, 79, 99, 100, 101, 105, 107
'innocent' eye(s) (ears) 107
  myth of the 43
institutional character of art 35, 37
intellect and emotion 69–70
intellectual effort and aesthetic awareness (*see also* thinking) 50
intention(s) 40, 43–4, 51
intentional object(s) 54, 57, 87
interpretation(s), interpreting 18, 25, 48, 54, 56, 62, 68, 79, 99

*Intimations of Immortality Ode* (Wordsworth) 84
inventiveness 9, 71
*Ion* (Plato) 16
Italian Symphony (Mendelssohn) 62

Johnson, R. V. 17
jokes, joke-telling 30, 64, 88, 89
*Journey of the Magi* (Eliot) 56
judgement 19, 45, 47, 88, 92, 96, 109
  value 93
justification of aesthetic appraisals, judgements 12, 61–5, 68, 92, 96, 97

Kandinsky, W. 80
Kant, I. 17, 18, 113
Keats, J. 81
Kennick, W. 65
'knowing that' 50, 85
knowledge (*see also* understanding) 5, 16, 25, 41, 43, Ch. 4 *passim*, Ch. 5 *passim*, 99, 102, 104, 106
  acquaintance- (experiential) 87
  practical 79
  propositional 50, 85

Laban, R. 70
*Lamentation* (Graham) 94
Langer, S. K. 83
language(s) (*see also* vocabulary, word(s)) 7, 9, 10, 41, 42, 78, 81–3
  aesthetic use of 91–2
  everyday (ordinary) 12–13, 33, 91
learning and aesthetic awareness 55, 75, 101
  and art 7, 9, 42, 56, 72, 75, 83, 85, 87, 91, 101
*Let's Make an Opera* (Britten) 30
Lillee, D. 104
linguistic skills 3, 10
literature 2–3, 10, 17, 21, 23, 31, 45, 55–7, 81, 87, 94
'literature and the fine arts' 3, 25
Lloyd, C. 105

Macbeth 52
make-believe 22, 49
making and doing 2, 6–8, 11, 73, 93, 94–5
Meager, R. 20, 27, 47, 60, 63
meaning(s) 11, 27, 33, 55–6, 57, 64, 74, 81, 83, 99
'meaning-embodied' 83–4

# INDEX

medium, media (of art) 40, 74, 78, 82, 108
Meeson, P. 70, 75
Mendelssohn, F. 62
mental abilities, capacities 9, 71–2
  faculty of 'taste' 17
  images 46, 47, 50, 51, 52
  states 54, 80, 91
mode(s) (categories) of awareness, experience 5, 11, 24
Moore, H. 86
moral and aesthetic appraisal(s), awareness 4, 5, 9, 10, 23, 37, 65, 66, 76, 102, 109
  development 9–10, 76
  education 66
  good and beauty 16
Morris-Jones, H. 82–3
movement, moving 2, 4, 22, 43, 103, 104
  to music 75
*Movement: Physical Education in the Primary Years* (DES) 82
Mozart, W. A. 74
*Mulberry Bush, The* (Calder) 62
Munch, E. 80
Murdoch, I. 22, 76
music 2, 5, 6, 10, 15, 30, 31, 36, 45, 52, 56, 68, 78, 80, 82, 86, 91, 92, 94, 95, 103, 107, 108, 112
  moving to 75

Naish, M. 33
nature, aesthetic appreciation of 3, 17, 28–9, Ch. 6 *passim*
Newton, I. 23, 40
non-aesthetic concepts 5
  qualities 20
notational symbols 91
*Noye's Fludde* (Britten) 30

Oakeshott, M. 88
'objectivist' theories in aesthetics 20–1, 64
objectivity and aesthetic appraisals 19, 46
*objets trouvés* 31, 40
O'Connor, D. J. 73–4
Offenbach, J. 55
operas 30
originality 43, 72, 81
*Orpheus in the Underworld* (Offenbach) 55
Orton, J. 7
Osborne, H. 34, 60
outdoor pursuits 103

painting(s) 2, 5, 6, 22, 27, 32, 35, 43, 78, 79, 80, 98, 107, 108
parents 30, 106, 108
participant enjoyment 73
participation 6, 7–8, 73, 104
Pater, W. 68
perception(s), perceiving 16, 18–21, 38, Ch. 4 *passim*, 68, 81, 87, 90–1, 96, 100, 101, 103
performances, performing 73, 74, 76, 80, 87, 91, 95, 104, 105
performer(s) 15, 46, 65, 78, 79, 92, 104
performing arts 6, 68, 87
persons and art 60, 86–7, 90, 96
personal relationships 10–11
Pevsner, N. 46
Phenix, P. 83
philosophy, philosophical inquiry 11–12, 24, 27, 111–13
  of art 14–15, 110
photography 106
physical education 2, 103, 104
Pinter, H. 7, 99
Plato 16, 70
play, play activities 30, 58, 69, 70
plays 5, 10, 29, 31, 36, 57
pleasure (*see also* delight, enjoyment, satisfaction) 6, 22, 42, 46, 53, 54, 57, 58, 104–5
poem(s), poetry 2, 5, 7, 32, 36, 37, 52, 55–6, 72, 81, 85, 86, 87, 95, 98, 107
  Georgian 39
*Poetics* (Aristotle) 16
Pole, D. 105
post-modern art, 25–8, 29
practical activity, activities 6, 7, 68–9
  knowledge 79
preference(s) 11, 12, 19, 39, 63, 88, 108
*Primary Education in England* (DES) 2, 3
problem-solving 9, 71
progress (*see also* development) 45–6, 68, 95, 106
Proust, M. 86
purpose(s) 15, 55, 58, 105
'purposiveness without purpose' 58–9

quality, qualities
  aesthetic 18–21, 23, 91
  expressive 41
  moral and writing 56

radio 36, 37, 95, 106
  drama, plays 7, 31

rationality and aesthetic appraisal 62–6
  and imaginative thinking 49
Rauschenberg, R. 31
Read, H. 43, 69, 70, 71, 72, 80, 110
reading 'for pleasure' 6–7
'realize', 'realizing' 85, 101
reality 18, 27, 32, 49–50, 58, 59, 65
reason(s), reason-giving, reasoning 53, 62ff.
recognition, recognizing 21, 45, 48
recording 6, 56, 75, 107
Redfern, H. B. 46, 91
Reid, L. A. 25, 53, 83, 87, 88, 91, 95
response(s), responding 19, 21, 45, 52, 53, 54, Ch. 4 *passim*, 87, 89, 90, 91, 93, 94, 97, 106, 108
riddles, riddle-posing 30, 88
Rogers, L. R. 91
Romanticism 80
Rosebury, B. J. 57
rules 16, 59, 60, 81, 83

satisfaction (*see also* delight, enjoyment, pleasure) 15, 21, 23, 53, 84, 104
Saw, R. 10, 56, 88, 99
Schaper, E. 16, 57, 71, 92
Schiller, J. F. C. 70–1, 110, 113
Schoenberg, A. 80
school assembly 2, 103
  building(s) 4, 109
  environment 109
  uniform 3
science, scientific awareness (thinking) 5, 37, 49–50, 71
Scruton, R. 4, 13, 15, 21, 49, 56, 66, 79, 81, 87
sculpture(s) 6, 36, 38, 78, 91, 100, 107
seeing as (*see also* experiencing as) 46, 48, 50, 51
self, the 22, 76, 77
  -advancement 66
  -assessment 76, 94
  -criticism 94
  -deception 90
  -expression 80
  -realization 9, 80
sensation(s) 3, 19, 50, 53, 54, 103
sense impressions 18, 48
sensory awareness, experience 17, 55
sensuous experience(s), response(s) 3, 22, 75
  pleasure 23
Shakespeare, W. 74

Sibelius, J. 52
Sibley, F. N. 20, 21, 63
Simpson, A. 1
singing, songs 15, 30, 68, 79
  folk 76
Sircello, G. 79, 99, 101
skill(s) (*see also* craftsmanship, technique(s)) 11, 15, 60, 72, 75, 77, 84, 87, 91, 93, 95, 104–5, 107
  linguistic 3, 10
  bodily 10
  social 3, 10
skilfulness 103
socio-historical character of art 35ff., 82
Southwell Minster 46
spectators 73, 104–5
spontaneity 43, 44, 77, 82
'spontaneous overflow of powerful feelings' 32
sport(s) 9, 62, 104–5
standards 6, 12, 41, 42, 48, 61, 75, 94, 107
Stevenson, C. L. 33
Stewart, D. 33
stories 5, 22, 30, 59, 75
Strawson, P. F. 24, 28, 73
structure(s), structuring 58, 86
style(s) 40, 43, 81, 95, 104, 108
  hair- 109
subjective character of aesthetic awareness (*see also* aesthetic feeling) 19, 66
supposing (*see also* entertaining a thought, thinking) 46, 52
Symes, C. 84

taste 17, 61, 63, 65, 88
teacher(s) 11, 68, 77, 79, 89, 90, 92, 106, 108
  -education 93, 110
teaching Chs. 5 and 6 *passim*
technical ability 15
technical details, terms 64, 89, 91
technique(s) (*see also* skill(s)) 11, 40, 76, 77, 78, 83
television 7, 30, 36, 95, 106
  plays 31, 62
theories, accounts of the aesthetic Ch. 2 *passim*, 89, 101, 109–110
  of art Ch. 3 *passim*
  of human development 43
  of education 43
thinking, thought(s) 37–8, 46, 49–50, 52, 64, 70, 71, 82, 83, 84, 96

# INDEX

Tormey, A. 78
tradition(s) and art 36, 41, 43, 81, 82, 98
tragedy 31, 57–8
training 9, 60, 71–2
truth 2, 46, 49, 56, 62, 81

ugliness, ugly 4, 5, 17, 18, 19, 47
'ugly' 19, 67
understanding (*see also* knowledge) 9–10, 16, 49, 55, 63, 65, 79, 80, 85ff., 96, 106
 aesthetic 5, 85ff.
 interpersonal 9, 10, 11, 102
uniqueness 60
unity 60, 95–6, 108
Urmson, J. O. 24

value(s) 10, 12, 41, 56, 65, 75, 92, 94
vocabulary, vocabularies (*see also* language, words) 81, 84, 91, 105

*Walking Away* (Day Lewis) 86
Warhol, A. 28
Weitz, M. 33
Weston, M. 86
White, J. P. 8, 68, 69, 102
Wigman, M. 77
Wilde, O. 18
Wilson, J. 9, 76, 88
*Winter's Tale, The* (Shakespeare) 95
Wittgenstein, L. 33, 34, 35, 36, 41, 54, 81, 87
Wollheim, R. 24, 28, 73
word(s) 36, 38, 55–6, 59, 67, 78, 82, 83, 84, 86
 aesthetic use of (*see also* language, vocabulary) 19–21
Wordsworth, W. 32, 84, 101

Yeats, W. B. 89